Shantè T. Hanks

TITANIUM WOMAN

MY SURVIVAL

MY SCARS

MY STORY

SHANTÈ T. HANKS

Shantè T. Hanks

Titanium Woman Copyright © 2015 Shantè T. Hanks

For information address Carpè Diem Publishing, a division of HMG, LLC, P.O. Box 1219, Bridgeport, CT 06601 or www.shantehanks.com

Front/Back Cover Photography & Cover Theme:
Derek Blanks of Derek Blanks Photography

Cover Layout: Lloyd Bromfield of Brom Design Group

Front/Back Makeup: Sìmone M. Turner
of DEMO Makeup Artistry

ISBN:1511415371
ISBN-13:9781511415378

*In dedication to my mother, sister and family &
friends who were there for me then and now.
Thank you. You are all gems.*

*To my Nana who instilled my strength and
conviction of knowing anything is possible.
Can't means not able and I am able to do anything.
She is my angel,
always watching over me from above.*

Thank you to all the apples in my orchard.

Shantè T. Hanks

TABLE OF CONTENTS

Shantè T. Hanks

FOREWARD

When first asked to be a part of this masterful endeavor, for a brief moment I became a little teary eyed at the invitation, you see I was overflowing with joy to think that I was thought of enough to take part in something so wonderful and of this magnitude as I am honored yet humbled. You see, there is a very strong connection between the Author and I as I have known her all of her life. I have witnessed her maturation from adolescence to adulthood.

Shantè has always had an unquenchable thirst for knowledge. She's always been a go getter, a glass half full person, the consummate optimist. She would always inquire as to why not. She has always been a critical thinker with a very creative mind and sense of self.

This pen to paper memoir that you are about to embark on is a true and accurate account of a very sobering event of many years ago. The ensuing pages depict the courage, determination, will-power and above all and most important, the faith, which encompasses all the above mentioned attributes that go into this mastery work of words that is going to touch some readers life whether directly or indirectly.

It is truly my honor and pleasure to be part of what I feel is sure to be an awesome read, that is sure to lift your spirits and give you the unshakeable desire to know that you can; to be that "why not?"

Arthur E. Cauthen II

ACKNOWLEDGMENTS

Dr. Howard Rankin
Couldn't have done this without you.

Pastor Bennett
Thank you for everything.

Sadia Douglas
You are unwavering...a true friend indeed.

Arthur E. Cauthen, II
Thank You Uncle Gene.

Thank you to the State Police Troopers, Emergency Responders and Doctors who were on call that fateful night:

Dr. Michael Ivy
I thank God for you.
Thank you for letting him use you to save me.

Dr. Rolf Langeland
Thank you for putting Humpty Dumpty back together again. I thank God for your ingenuity & perseverance. in knowing you could build me back piece by piece.

Officer Johnston
Thank God you were first on the scene.

Sergeant Lynch
Thank you for going the extra mile.

Dr. Henderson
Thank you for listening.

Lloyd Bromfield
Thank you for being there when it counted.

INTRODUCTION

Whether it be sickness, hard times, weddings or funerals, people notice who shows up...and who does not.

My experience strengthened my faith in God.
He showed up! I know that if it were not for God keeping me, strengthening me and healing me, I would not be the survivor I am, sharing my story and showing my scars.

After reading this book, your first take away should be **Do Not Drink And Drive!** After that, if you don't remember anything else, remember to be sure to acknowledge those that are there for you and support you through your life's journey. Be sure to let them know how much you value them. Be sure to let your family and friends know how much you love them. Tomorrow is not promised. Every moment that you get to share with them is a gift. My dad, uncle and aunt have passed on since my Carpè Diem gathering. I cherish the time I got to spend with each of them.

I wrote this book to tell my story and maybe inspire you to tell yours. I hope it resonates something within you. Telling your story may not be writing a book but finding your voice so you can find your happiness. You may not have a tragic occurrence that you can identify with but if you're not living each day of your life to the fullest, loving you and happy with what you do, then it is tragic.
If reading my book emotes something within you or ignites a dormant flame inside of you, then I have accomplished my goal.

Thank you for joining me on my journey.

Shantè T. Hanks

ONE

Carpè Diem

Seize the Day

"Gratitude is the sign of noble souls."
- Aesop

It was a sunny June day in 2009 in my hometown of Bridgeport, Connecticut. I had been thinking about it for a while and on this summer's day, I finally made my decision. Yes, I would do it. I'd never heard of anyone doing anything like this but, hey, I am used to thinking a little outside of the box.

I decided that I would take care of all of the arrangements. I have always had high levels of energy, been independent and resolute when I needed to be and so arranging a dinner party for about eighty people didn't faze me at all. In fact, I thought my biggest challenge would be curbing my mother's natural inclination to take charge. I might need her help with finding a suitable location and helping with the food, but aside from that, I'd try to keep the rest of the arrangements a secret, not just from her but the other guests as well .

In my mind, I started to construct the guest list. As I considered each name, the memories of each person didn't just return they exploded into my consciousness and brought with them immense feelings of warmth and love. A decade might have passed but the memories didn't just linger, they stood bolt upright and demanded attention, sometimes a little imperfect but always inspirational. Memory can be like that, imperfect yet inspiring, and it was one of the reasons I wanted to organize this celebration. I didn't want to ever forget what happened to me and the role every single one of my guests played in my life-defining moment.

Every year on the anniversary, I would receive lots of calls and text messages of love from my friends and family. This year, the ten year anniversary date actually fell on a Friday and I decided that I did not want to sacrifice authenticity for convenience. The date had become so significant for me that having the event on the actual day was not negotiable, even though, a Saturday rather than a Friday night might have been more convenient for some of my guests. I started to get really excited at the prospect of my gathering. I wanted it to be an evening of celebration but also one of gratitude. A time to reminisce, but also to reflect.

I told my mother about my plan but insisted that she need to do nothing. She was excited and, of course, very anxious to help but I firmly insisted that I would be doing this on my own.

She gave me that look, the one that suggested that I probably shouldn't give her any more details of my plans. I knew she would not make this easy for me because she likes to plan all our family events and "we must have favors." I hate favors! I call them dust catchers because she saves them from every wedding, every baby shower, every bridal shower, and every birthday. I am letting out a sigh of defeat because I can hear her voice in my head making the argument in favor of favors...She considers it improper to not have a customized favor when hosting an event. The only favors that make sense to me are edible so I compromised to keep the peace and had chocolate favors and allowed her to help with the menu and reserve the venue. Everything else was off limits!

My mother came through, of course. She reserved the West Haven Conference Center. This was a great choice. West Haven was just twenty minutes from Bridgeport and it held lots of fond memories for me -- I really like the town. Moreover, the Conference Center is a converted seafood restaurant--the old Harbor Mist-- and not only has great ambience and facilities but actually is located right on the water. And on a Friday evening in mid-September, the beach breezes were usually delightful.

The guest list really chose itself. It was simply a list of all those who were there *with* me and *for* me when it mattered most.

I did add a couple of my co-workers from my current workplace that weren't in my life when it so dramatically changed. The evening would give them a better insight into who I am and allow them to meet some of my family and longtime friends. Generally, however, I am a pretty private person and I don't easily mingle my professional life with my private life. I don't like to mix my worlds. Still, these relatively new co-workers were more than just colleagues and I wanted to invite them into my world, the one they could never have imagined. I also invited previous co-workers from the university; they were like family and some were on my list to thank. And, of course, I invited my current boyfriend, all 6'11" of him. He was sure to stand out. Oh how I love a tall man...

In many ways, the preparation required was similar to that needed for a wedding. I went shopping for a new cocktail dress and found one that I loved in my favorite color, garnet red, my birthstone. I also introduced the garnet color into the table settings and complimented the color with silver candlesticks and white floating candles on a mirrored base to reflect the lighting perfectly. *The devil is in the details*.

I covered all the details and ordered the necessary items including a DJ and 3 cases of *Sweet Bitch*, my favorite wine. Hate the name--so crass, but love the wine. That left just one item requiring immediate attention.

Initially, I knew the theme of the event was celebration and gratitude but now I had to design the invitations. The more I thought about it, the more one idea kept leaping out at me.

The events of September 19, 1999 had convinced me more than ever that life isn't about waiting, it's about living. It's about appreciating every moment. It's about showing up every day. It's about gratitude for having a day at all. With those thoughts in my mind, I devised the invitations, the title of which consisted of just two words -- Carpè Diem.

I produced the invitations and sent them on their way. They went to my grandmother "Gram" who was 86 yrs old and with my nephew, Justice, who was 7 yrs old. I would have the oldest to the youngest family members in the room, as well as about eighty other guests.

Some people called to happily accept their invitations and some asked "what kind of event is this", "what should I wear" and what those two words "carpè diem" mean?

My response was simply, "It means lots of things but one is that you must always remember to tell your loved ones that you love them." "I want to acknowledge people who I love," I added.

Summer turned into fall and it was soon September. On the day of the event, I spent the entire afternoon checking the venue and making sure everything was in place.

The old seafood restaurant, with a wall of windows facing the water, looked spectacular and just the way I had envisioned it. From the white candles to the ivory tablecloths, the room looked great! And that beach breeze was just delightful. I left satisfied that all was in order and made my way home to prepare myself for the big night.

Guests started to arrive at 7:45 p.m.. I always pick odd start times for my events; it ensures promptness. The idea was for my guests to mingle and relax before sitting down to dinner at which point I would make my grand entrance. My mother didn't quite appreciate this staging and as guests started to sit down for dinner she told them dinner would not be served until I arrived.

She called me on my cell phone in a panic.
"Where are you?" she asked frantically. "You need to get here now! Everyone wants to know where you are," which meant she wanted to know where I was and what was taking me so long to arrive.

I assured my mom that this was all part of my plan.
"Ma, this is what I wanted. Let them sit down and eat," I insisted.

I told my mother that once everyone was in their seats I would make my entrance. There was no need to call again and, in fact, another call would indeed make me late. At around 8:40 p.m. I entered the room.

I received a standing ovation. It was a magical moment. I was there with people who meant so much to me and they were there because I meant so much to them. It was an outpouring of love and memories.

As soon as I walked in, I picked up the microphone and started to do exactly what I had dreamt of doing for a long, long time. I went from person to person, introducing each one of them, telling them and all the assembled guests how important they were to me, and what they had done for me those ten years ago. Some of them were surprised that I had remembered, or even knew, so many of the details of their support. It wasn't just my favorite wine that was flowing. Fortunately, there were plenty of tissues available. Emotions were running high and deep.

As I went around the room introducing the guests and talking about their meaning in my life, they, of course, wanted to have their say, too. I was mindful of this and the fact that my ex-boyfriend, who wanted to participate, even though, we were both seeing other people but still friends, would soon have to leave to go to work.

So, he was one of the first people I acknowledged. In his response, he remembered our time together and then said, "Despite the fact that it has been almost three years since we broke up, I want you to know that I love you and always will." Awkward. Very awkward!

Cheers! I toasted my guests. Tonight was about them.

Even though, I knew this event would be a love fest, I wasn't quite prepared for those exact sentiments. When I got the microphone back, I was something that I rarely am -- lost for words. Fortunately, one of my girlfriends, Tameeka, stepped in and said something diplomatic while I regained my composure. I couldn't get the words out to acknowledge my current beau properly because my ex left me dumbfounded. My sister, Simone and my cousin, Robert applauded my ex's speech which made matters even worse and I think I was blushing too. I can really laugh about it now -- I was flattered but uncomfortable that night.

As you might expect, my current boyfriend, the really tall one, was a little upset about my former boyfriend's comments. He simmered a bit and later I couldn't see him anywhere. Let me assure you that when someone who is 6 feet 11 inches tall leaves the room, everyone notices. I found him sitting in his friend's car. He never drove himself anywhere so I knew he couldn't really leave but clearly we needed to talk, which we did.

I must admit I was very flattered by my ex's sentiments and secretly reveled in my current beau being jealous. Can't blame a girl for that.

The unintended consequence of this unfolding drama was that when I left the reception area, people followed me and so now half the party had migrated outdoors. Eventually, we went back inside and joined everyone on the dance floor. Apart from that episode, the evening was just fantastic. Everyone, well almost everyone, had a great time. They ate and they drank, they laughed and they danced. At one point everyone was actually line dancing -- yes, even some of my older aunts! I had everyone sign my Carpe Diem poster, a great memento of the event that I still treasure.

I never did get to eat any of the food that I had meticulously planned and prepared. Well, that's not quite true. I did manage to steal a bite of the exquisite red velvet cake imported directly from Brooklyn's own Cakeman Raven. My good girlfriend Sadia and her husband Greg personally delivered it. It was so good that people are still talking about it today, five years later.

I have lots of wonderful memories of that evening and many great photos. Some of the people who were there that night are no longer with us, like my wonderful Stepfather, Barry but I call him "Pops". Pops meant, and means, so much to me.

Also my Uncle Kevin "Kebby" was with us that evening but has since has passed away. I lost them just nine days apart.

Kebby passed January 12th, 4 days before my birthday and my Dad passed January 21st, just five days after. They are both truly in my heart and confirm the reason behind my Carpè Diem party.

I am so happy I made the decision to arrange and host that evening. Everyone who was there will always be with me, an essential part of my story, integral to my life.

The fact that I didn't discard the idea and invested the time, money and energy is testimony to the fact that I believe with all my heart that life is for living and that love and gratitude should never be delayed or even second-guessed. It can be summed up in two simple words -- Carpè Diem -- Seize the Day!

TWO

Destiny

"It is a mistake to look too far ahead. The chain of destiny can only be grasped one link at a time."
- Winston Churchill

It was the summer of 1999 and it was hot! Despite just having completed my Master of Education Degree at Southern Connecticut State University, I was still on campus because I had a full time position as a Hall Director in the Housing Department. I even had to stay during the long hot weeks of summer as the university hosted numerous sports teams and organized Resident Advisor Training. My summer fun was always cut short due to the sports camps starting in August. Although, I didn't mind football camp so much but it was extremely hot this particular summer and there was no air conditioning in my office. Only the Housing main office and newer buildings had A/C.

It was so hot this summer! I was reminded of my days as a student at Clark Atlanta University. Being from Connecticut, I had never felt days as hot and humid as August in Atlanta. But, I loved ATL!

However, there was one steamy hot day here in Connecticut that in response to soaring temperatures and to save on energy costs, the Governor shut down all state institutions.

And this particular day happened to be Thursday; pay day! I called my cousin, Kellie, who also worked for the State and close by the university. I said, "Let's blow this popsicle stand!" I have no idea the origin of that phrase but I always heard my mother say it and it tickles me.

Kellie was my "road dog" as they say. We have been close since we were little. We celebrated every birthday together with my younger sister, Simone and our other cousins Teasha, Shonda and Kellie's younger sister, Kiese. Kellie, Teasha and I were cheerleaders on our high school squad together; "Go Central Hilltoppers!" Kellie is two years older and Teasha and I are four months apart in age.

Kellie and I were both excited about our unexpected day off. I offered to pick her up in my Acura Coupe. I had an amethyst Acura CL. It was my third car but the first I bought brand new, fresh off the lot! It had all the bells and whistles I could want. It was loaded--gray leather heated seats, sunroof, Bose system and 6 disc CD changer in dash. I loved driving that car.

Freed from the tyranny of work, we headed off to Bloomingdales in White Plains. I had been eyeing a pair of Fendi sandals in their shoe department. They were too cute but almost $200! Was I ready to start buying $200 sandals? I knew this would be a slippery slope but it was payday and we had a free afternoon to go have fun and shop.

I felt the shoe Gods were telling me "Buy them!" We had a lot of fun and of course, I bought the cute, Fendi sandals.

The summer turned out to be eventful. Shortly after our unexpected day off, my nephew Jeremiah was born. He was in the hospital at Yale and I was dying to see him. The only problem was that as a Hall Director it was difficult to leave the campus. There were regulations about when I could and couldn't leave and I had to maintain an almost constant presence on campus. But when I learned that Jeremiah had struggled through a tough delivery and was actually in the Pediatric Intensive Care Unit at Yale, struggling for his life, I was determined nothing was going to stop me. He was less than 3 miles away from the campus. I snuck out after midnight and made my way into the Yale Children's Hospital where I saw him.

I had never spent any time in an intensive care unit and was amazed at all the gadgetry and technology on display. I hoped that I would never have a need to be in ICU again. My nephew actually seemed to be responding to the treatment and in fact, he made a great recovery and went home with my sister.

The summer wore on. School was back in session and I was looking forward to the semester.

Now, I was qualified to teach History and Social Sciences to middle and high school students. My student teaching assignments had been interesting.

My student teacher coordinator was a hard-nosed Marine who decided to assign this young black teacher to an affluent school in Prospect near Waterbury. I thought it was a terrible placement as I had envisaged teaching in a more urban environment. But here I was, headed to teach eighth grade history in a school where there were no black students, teachers or administrators. In fact, I think I was the first black teacher in the school's history. As I say this, I'm hoping I'm incorrect but I don't think so. Although, I don't mind being *the first* but the thought of being a pioneer for teaching at a public school in Connecticut in these modern times, is not want I thought would be a great accomplishment but I'll take it!

It turned out to be a great experience. It gave me a sense of the scope of education. I hope I taught them well. I learned some stuff, too. One day, a student volunteered that he would have to make up a quiz for my class. He said. "Ms. Hanks, I won't be here for the quiz tomorrow."

"Why are you going to miss the quiz?" I asked.

"My dad's flying me into the city in our private plane."

Enough said.

The students had laptops that would be the envy of most of my college friends and Fridays everyone got pizza from Pizza Hut.

I mean the kids actually had pizza from Pizza Hut every Friday for lunch. As much as I enjoyed teaching middle students the fact is that I prefer teaching college students. There was a wider age range and just generally more diversity and flexibility.

I slipped into my fall semester routine. Working out was always part of my life and this year was no exception. I had been enjoying kickboxing for some time. I was kicking the bag and sparring with partners but now there was a changing landscape that had me thinking about taking this activity in a different direction.

Female boxing had been around for a while but now, with the entry of Laila Ali, the great Muhammad Ali's daughter, there seemed to be more interest in the sport. I was a huge fan of Ali, the world champion. I saw him as an inspirational figure and he was a true hero to me. Plus we are both Capricorns -- a day apart in fact. In addition to Laila, George Foreman's daughter was also considering throwing her hat into the ring. I spoke to a boxing trainer at the gym next door to my mother's job about the potential growth of female boxing and I was definitely interested. We arranged to attend Laila Ali's next fight at a casino in New York scheduled for October. We also set up my training schedule and planned to start my training the following week. I was about to learn the ropes. It was September 15th.

The following Saturday, I had a special event. It was my cousin Val's bridal shower. This was a great opportunity to see virtually all the female members of my family on the Shepard side. I had a busy life and didn't get to see many of them much. Most of them hadn't seen me since we had our last Shepard Family Reunion at Gram's house. They all knew my world revolved around education and Southern. I hoped I was being an inspiration and role model to some of the younger members of my family.

Because of my interest and comfort with public speaking, I was often volunteered by my mother and aunts to be the hostess at family events and this was no exception. I didn't mind though, Val and I have always been close. This was going to be a long day followed by plans to go to The Roxy nightclub in Norwalk with the girls. I bought a brand new all black outfit – short trouser skirt with matching blouse to match but not upstage my new Fendi Sandals and Victoria's Secret apparel -- and headed off to the West Haven Conference Center. Let the festivities begin!

It was a great event. I got a chance to catch up with my fam. On one side, there are the Shepards, who are my Pop's family. Pop's is Barry, my stepfather but he's been in my life since I was about six years old and the Shepards are *my* family. On the other side are the Hanks, the family of my biological dad. He and my mom divorced when I was very young. I'm close to them as well.

At Val's shower I got a chance to hang out with my cousins but was looking forward to going out with Kellie and the girls later. The weather was great and because my summer was cut short due to life on campus, I couldn't wait to go out and enjoy this beautiful last weekend of summer.

Teasha decided not to come out with us so Kellie, Shonda and I headed off to The Roxy. When we got there, however, there was a huge line to get in. Nightclubs close at 2:00 a.m. in Connecticut so we weren't too thrilled about waiting to get in. We decided to head to another club in Stamford. When we got there, it was clear that all our friends and real action was back in Norwalk. "What should we do? " I asked.

By now it was about 1:00 a.m.. Kellie wasn't too keen about heading back to anywhere but home. I could see her point. I was ready to call it a night too, head home, watch a little TV and maybe even get a chance to play with my nephew, Jeremiah, who was now one month old. We decided to call it a night.

I dropped the girls off and headed to my parents' house. Jeremiah was asleep but my mother was still awake so we chatted as I told her about the night's events. Some time shortly after I got home, I fell asleep watching *Showtime at the Apollo* with my mother and nephew.

The next thing I know, my mom was shaking me to wake me up.

"Shaney! It's three o'clock, don't you have to be back on campus? You need to leave!" my mother said.

"Oh Shoot!" I don't have a pass to stay out overnight and I have to be back on campus no later than three. It was already three! I jumped up, picked up the keys to my car and rushed out the door.

It was about a twenty minute drive to campus but I wasn't too concerned about the time. I just wanted to get there safely. I drove cautiously as the area was known for deer and the last thing I needed was a deer running at my headlights.

About a half mile from home I entered the Merritt Parkway that would speed me back to campus. It was six minutes past three in the morning on September 19, 1999.

As I entered the parkway, someone was exiting it. The only problem was that he was exiting the parkway the wrong direction and was headed straight for me. I never had time to react or even consider that life would never be the same again.

He hit me head on!

THREE

Crash

Luck is a very thin wire between survival and disaster and not many people can keep their balance on it.
- Hunter Thompson

I was driving my car onto the Merritt Parkway. It was the first brand new car I had ever bought. My previous car, a candy apple red Mitsubishi Eclipse with cloth seats and no air conditioning, I had given to my sister.

A few weeks earlier near this spot, a college student from Brazil, Rodrigo, had been stopped one afternoon for going the wrong way onto an exit ramp. Rodrigo was a twenty year-old student at Western Connecticut State University in Danbury. He and his mother had come to the U.S. from Brazil to register him for school but his mother had since returned to her home country. The police gave Rodrigo a ticket and a warning.

Now, as I headed onto the parkway I saw a Mitsubishi Eclipse heading straight for me. It wasn't a deer, which was always a concern when driving on the Merritt Parkway especially at night. It was Rodrigo!

It all happened in an instant. I think I remember seeing lights right in front of me but honestly my memory of that moment is an unreliable blur. Rodrigo hit me head on. The impact drove my car onto the embankment. Rodrigo was driving right at me going the wrong way and hit me so hard, that I was now facing the wrong direction on the highway. My car was on the embankment but could go over the side into the water at any time. Not that the car was functional. For one thing, the engine wasn't where it should be any longer. Forced by the impact out of its usual and customary position, the hot engine landed in my lap. Well not so much landed, as crushed into it.

The collapse of the front of the car meant that I took the full force of the buckling machinery. My pelvis was shattered. My knees were smashed and burned. My wrists were broken and my ankles were crushed. And those were the least of my injuries.

Rodrigo wasn't so fortunate. He was not wearing a seatbelt. The force of the impact ejected him through his windshield and out onto the unforgiving concrete. He must have died instantly.

I was conscious but I was in pain and in shock.

Officer Linda Johnston was the first one on the scene, which was remarkable for two reasons. First, she was the only black, female State Trooper in the state of Connecticut. Second, she was a nurse by training.

When Trooper Johnston reached me she must have been relieved to see that I was still alive and conscious. As a nurse, she knew to try to keep me conscious and so she asked me a lot of questions. She was trying to keep me engaged and distracted as she waited for the arrival of backup and the emergency medical services.

"Are you all right? Are you in pain?" She asked.

"Well, I'm alive but I am not all right." I responded. Little did I know how bad I was.

Trooper Johnson's questions continued. What's my name? Where am I from? Where was I going? She worked hard to keep me conscious. I was conscious all right. Never one to be shy about expressing my views, I offered a question of my own.

"Can you please stop asking me all these questions and get this engine off of me?" I pleaded. This must have gone on for what felt like forever.

I don't remember much after that. Actually, I don't remember that either. This is what I was later told. I know the Stratford EMTs and Fire Department used the Jaws of Life to extricate me from my car.
And I am sure after examining me, the paramedics were very careful how they moved me into the ambulance. Eventually, I was on my way to Bridgeport Hospital. After that, I must have lost

consciousness and it would be a while before I would regain it.

Thank God, even though, I lived on Southern's campus for years, I never changed my address on my driver's license. Once I was removed from the car, Trooper Johnston was able to get to the back seat and retrieve my purse. There she found my driver's license -- and my parent's address on Clover Hill.

Linda Johnston did not need to go to my mother's house and break the news to my parents. There were others whose job that was but she decided that she wanted to be the one to tell my mother that her daughter was in critical condition. She had a daughter my age and felt a connection to me. Johnston accompanied the ambulance to the hospital and watched and waited until I was transferred into medical care. Once I was admitted and Linda got a sense of what was happening, she headed out to my parents' house.

It was three hours after the accident, at about six on Sunday morning, when she pulled up outside the house. She approached the door and rang the bell.
My mother knew something was wrong because my grandmother, Nana, came to her in the middle of the night and said, "She's going to be ok."

My mother didn't know what she meant at the time but she knew something terrible happened because I hadn't called. It was my customary practice to call whenever I was headed home just to reassure my mother that I had reached my destination and was safe. She said to Jeremiah, even though, he was only a baby, "I'm going to get your aunt for not calling when she got home."

My mother had a sinking feeling. Now, pulling back the curtains of the bay window in the living room, she could see the police car, a sure sign that I wasn't safe. She didn't want to open the door. You don't have to accept the reality if you don't allow yourself to hear it. Life is still normal and good but as soon as you open that door, everything changes.

She ran to get my dad. The doorbell awakened my sister, Simone. Holding Jeremiah, Simone answers the door to Trooper Johnston. Trooper Johnston first confirmed she has the correct address and that I in fact lived there. Simone confirmed she was at the right house.

"There's been an accident," she started. By now my parents hear this and my dad asks "How bad is it?" And seeing the look on the trooper's face he quickly added, "Is she alive?"

Now my mother wants to hear.

Trooper Johnston continues answering my dad's question. "She was alive when I left the hospital," said the trooper, honestly if not reassuringly.

"But you need to get there as soon as possible," Johnston added as my mother moves closer. Then, looking at my parents who were now standing together she said, "She's a fighter." She quickly told them my response to her questions when she was trying to keep me conscious till the ambulance and fire department arrived.

At this point, my sister and parents are together hearing this information. I am sure Simone wanted to go to the hospital but she had her young baby to care for. Life suddenly seemed all the more precious.

My parents scrambled around in a sickened panic, collected their wits, thoughts and keys, and headed out the door.

When my mother and stepfather arrived at the hospital they rushed to the front desk in a panic asking for me. The nurses wouldn't give my parents any information at first. The staff acted as if they didn't know what my father was talking about and they did not have a *Shantè Hanks* at the hospital as a patient. My father, who is always calm and rational, had hit his breaking point.

"What's going on? Where is my daughter!" He demanded.

They finally told him they had a Jane Doe that fit my description and they needed to confirm the information. While this was happening, no one would tell my parents whether I am alive or not.

My father demanded to know why they had me listed as a Jane Doe when they had my license, could confirm the car registration and State Trooper Johnston confirmed my identity? Finally, after what probably took ten minutes but seemed to take a lifetime, they confirmed I was in fact the Jane Doe that had been brought to the hospital and was involved in the fatal car accident on the Merritt Parkway.

A nurse told my parents I was in surgery and directed them to the surgical waiting area. I had been in surgery for almost two hours already.

There was another woman waiting there. Her son had a heart attack and she was waiting for him to come out of surgery, too. She shared with my mother that her son had a bad heart from substance abuse.

Time ticked relentlessly but painstakingly on. My parents started to call family members to tell them what had happened. Some of those people had been with me no more than twelve hours earlier. Then I had been vibrant and alive, now I was comatose and hanging on by a thread.

My mother and the other woman waited, undeniably and inextricably connected by a bond that neither wanted. Their worlds had been turned upside down that night and now all they could do was wait and pray. And soon prayer walked through the door.

The priest's arrival freaked my mom out. He symbolized a possibility that she was obsessively trying to push from her mind. He didn't represent comfort but the sheer, horrific, sickening chance of her daughter's death. She moved as far away from him as possible.

The priest sensed her discomfort and tried to reassure her. He immediately addressed a dark, malicious thought that had been growing with an accelerated speed since the priest walked in.

"I don't know anything more than you do," he said. "I'm here because I've been told there are two patients in surgery and their families are in need of comfort. I'm here to pray with you. I am sorry if I scared you."

They prayed.

It had been more than two hours now since my parents had arrived at the hospital. Every time a door opened, their hearts jumped. But no doctors or surgeons were coming through that door; nurses, other hospital workers and then, family members.

As the morning wore on, my relatives arrived to join the vigil. One by one, family came to the hospital not only in hopes of seeing me but also to support my parents. Friends started coming as well. My mother called the campus to report what happened. When word got around, all my friends came around.

It was now midday. I had been in surgery for at least six hours and my parents had been there for four. Then there was some activity; a rise in energy that alerted everyone that something was about to happen. It was indeed. Morning was about to become mourning.

The other woman, who had been waiting so patiently for news of her son, was approached by a somber looking nurse. She was taken to some private area but there was no need to hear the conversation. It was clear that her son had died.

I can only imagine my parents' mixed emotions. "I am glad that wasn't us but I'm guilty that I am glad that it wasn't us. Will it be us?" Reality just got harsher.

Time edged glacially along. Now it was afternoon. More friends and relatives arrived and they were a help. Little did they know that this was going to be the first of many trips to the hospital for almost all of them. All of them, more than fifty by now, would have been reassured to know that at the time, but no one knew anything. And time moved on.

Around 5:00pm, after my parents had waited for ten hours, there was more activity. The doctor emerged.

My mother was struck by how young he looked. His red hair didn't help his professional appearance. He was actually in his late thirties. Dr. Michael Ivy.
My mother said he reminded her of the character "Opie". Ron Howard's role when he was younger on the Any Griffith Show.

Dr. Ivy gave my parents the news. I had several critical injuries that had been the focus of surgery. My left femur had been broken and needed urgent attention as the femoral artery was critical for survival. My lung had been punctured and I had internal bleeding around my spleen. My insides had been opened up by the doctor and would remain so for a while to allow for internal hemorrhage to release. The other injuries -- the pelvis fractured in five places, the broken wrists, smashed knees and fractured ankles weren't life-threatening and could be treated later.

"She's not out of the woods by any means," the doctor added. Then, he answered the inevitable question.

"She's got about a 40% chance of making it."

FOUR

Coma

If you're going through hell, keep going
- Winston Churchill

It had taken me five years to complete my undergraduate degree, mostly because I transferred to two different colleges in the middle of my undergraduate studies. I started at the University of Bridgeport, transferred to Clark Atlanta University, then finished at Southern Connecticut State University.

There were some undergraduate classes I did not like. I thought all electives that I had to take but were not part of my major; subjects like gym were a waste of time and money. I never understood why I had to take two years of gym. While at Clark we were able to cross-register at any school in the AUC. Oh, how I really wanted to fulfill my gym requirement by taking bowling at Spelman. No such luck though--class was always full.

But I navigated my way through all the necessary courses and requirements, got my degree and then wanted to continue with further studies. I was in no rush to be a responsible adult. I loved living on campus. I wanted to be a professional student.

Everyone told me that I would love graduate school because there were no damn electives! I would get to focus on my subject area and have more autonomy when choosing my classes. No more useless core requirements! *Dance Break!* A simple Cabbage-Patch will do.

I was offered a job in the Housing Department as a Graduate Intern. This came with an apartment, a stipend as well as free tuition. Shortly after, I was able to get a job as a Hall Director. This effectively made me a state employee with great medical benefits. I was now on a full time-time salaried status, in the union and I got an even larger apartment plus free tuition! Thank God my mother was a City employee so I had her medical benefits until 25 but dental ran out at 19. But as a Hall Director, I was set!

I probably go to the dentist more than any other doctor. I have always had sensitive teeth. I remember having a dream while an undergrad that my teeth were falling out! I was so scared because superstition says dreaming your teeth are falling out means you're going to die. I made my cousin, Robert, who also lived on campus stay with me in my townhouse. I was the Resident Advisor for the Townhouses on campus at the time. I say I'm not superstitious but tend to allow myself to get worked up over the silliest things. At least I used to.

Anyway, I took a couple of classes a week in grad school and worked my way through the curriculum. It is now late July, 1999 and I had been taking graduate classes year round for a while. One particular day I was looking at a form designed to help graduate students like me determine how many more credits were needed to fulfill the requirements of the master's degree. It was called a CEPR Form, Course Evaluation Program Requirement form.

As I pondered the courses I had taken and the ones that were available, there seemed to be something wrong. Each time I checked, however, I came up with the same answer. No matter how hard it was for me to fathom, the conclusion was inescapable. I had met all my requirements for my master's degree!

In some disbelief I shared my conclusion with my professor and academic advisor, Dr. Greengross, and we agreed to meet. When we met, he confirmed, "You're done." I was so excited! I just had to wait to receive official confirmation of my grades and then I could graduate. In all likelihood my graduation wouldn't be until May of 2000, but I could surely start planning.

My friends and family were shocked when I told them that I had got my Master's degree. They were thrilled, and surprised. Well my family was, I really didn't tell my friends, they just kind of found out. I'm pretty modest when it comes to certain things.

Completing my master's was so easy that I didn't bother bragging about it. I lived on campus and didn't have to pay for it. It was just a natural progression for me.

Most, like me, didn't know that I was so close to finishing. I told them that I was waiting for my transcripts to say *"Graduate Program Complete"* in order to be officially recognized and then I would feel different---I think. Little did I know how different I would be when those grades were finally delivered.

My grades arrived at my parents' house when I was in my coma. It was ironic. Here were my grades confirming that I had just obtained my Master of Education Degree while the doctors were questioning whether I would ever be anything more than a vegetable.

After a couple of days in Surgical Intensive Care Unit (SICU) the doctors were fairly sure I would make it physically. They just didn't know what shape I would be in mentally when I emerged from my coma. And I wasn't about to do that any time soon.

Not that I knew much about it, but my first few days in the hospital were spent undergoing surgical repair of my shattered body. The first surgery was for my femur and the protection of my femoral artery. Two days later I was back in surgery for the repair of my broken bones.

The repair to my smashed ankles, wrists and forearm took another seven hours. Five days later, I once again had major surgery, this time on my pelvis, which was broken in five places.

Dr. Ivy suggested to my mother, that she allow Dr. Langeland, a young orthopedic surgeon, who works in sports medicine, conduct the surgery on my shattered pelvis. Dr. Langeland showed my mother a handmade sketch of how he would put me back together if she allowed him to perform my surgery.

Now my mother was faced with a dilemma. The orthopedic surgeon who was on call the night of the accident had repaired my femur and inserted a titanium rod in my thigh. He anticipated performing the surgery on my pelvis as well. However, he told my mother I would have a limp and may need a special orthotic shoe because I will likely be permanently imbalanced.

Dr. Langeland assured my mother he could perform the surgery and I would walk regularly again and not need a special orthotic shoe. My mother was confused because the first doctor was advocating strongly for himself to do this surgery and he had recently performed surgery on my Uncle Mark but Dr. Langeland's confidence and Dr. Ivy's recommendation convinced my mother to go with Dr. Langeland and I couldn't be happier.

During my coma, there were times when I felt agitated and apparently I tried to remove the tubes from the various parts of my body. I do remember imagining my accident. I say imagining my accident because, in my mind, I visualized that the other driver was a 50 year-old drunk construction worker. Of course, I knew nothing about Rodrigo but in my coma, my mind created that story. This is important because it raises an important misconception about what is a coma.

A coma doesn't mean you are brain dead. There are two critical variables here: awareness and arousal. Awareness is the patient's response to outside stimuli. Does the patient respond to different sensory stimulation? Do they respond to a painful stimulus? Can they open their eyes? Awareness requires higher cognitive functioning.

Arousal concerns the level of activity in the brain. More primitive areas of the brain may show signs of life and that's important because they control critical life functions, like breathing. But even primitive brain arousal can lead to thoughts. Think of it like this, when you're in a deep sleep you're not very aware or maybe even responsive to the sounds going around you but you might be having a vivid dream.

So while I wasn't aware of my external environment, there was a lot going on in my head.

For example, I recall one nightmare in which a gang broke into my house and held me and my family hostage. It was the quintessential helplessness dream. On the other hand, I also imagined I was in a very peaceful place. It was all white and I met my grandmother, Nana, who had died several years earlier. I can't tell you whether this was heaven. It could have been. It definitely was a heavenly experience.

Back in the real world on earth, the doctors told my family that it would take a few weeks before they could allow me to awaken. I was in a medically induced coma due to the trauma my body endured.

The first week was spent in the surgeries. My mother was an ever-present by my bedside; she just wouldn't leave! But she had plenty of company.
I didn't know it but Pops, Daddy, my biological father up from Texas, aunts, uncles, friends and co-workers past and present, came by every day. They formed quite a crowd, which later would be an advantage for me. The visitors supported my mother as she waited patiently but anxiously at my side. I take that back, the part that I didn't know it--I could hear the voices of family and friends that came to my bedside and spoke to me. Even though, I was in a coma, I could hear voices.

My mother kept a detailed daily record of the medical events, which is actually a very smart thing to do for all sorts of reasons; advocacy, insurance, liability, and even memory.

You can imagine that the insurance issue was likely to be a major issue. My mother was getting extremely frustrated with it and, fortunately, now she had someone to turn to.

When my sister, Simone was eight, she was involved in a car accident. My mother was driving and loss consciousness. In fact, Simone's head was smashed against the windshield rendering her unconscious and eventually leaving a permanent scar, even after she had plastic surgery. An attorney was very helpful in helping my mother resolving the subsequent issues and my mother once again had to turn to the same attorney for yet another daughter involved in a car accident.

Tom had practically become an extended member of the family. Unfortunately, our relationship with Tom soured because he was negligent with my case. He was going through a divorce and missed a deadline to submit documents to the court. Dramshop laws have since changed, but in short, Tom dropped the ball and Rosemarie, a family friend, took over my case.

Another source of frustration for my mother was the wrecked body of my car. It was being held in a state trooper compound and couldn't be moved because it had been involved in an accident where there had been a fatality. Troop G is located on the outskirts of downtown Bridgeport.

The problem was that the location where the car was being stored was actually very visible from the Route 25 ramp off of I-95. Not only could the wrecked car easily be seen from the highway, it was also on the very route that my mother took from her home to the hospital when she didn't want to travel down Boston Avenue. Can you imagine that?

Each day, a mother is driving to the hospital not knowing whether her daughter is going to survive the day and on the way she has to see the wrecked car, a grisly reminder of the accident and my situation. Trooper Johnston intervened on our behalf and tried to get the car moved but until it was, my mother took a different route to the hospital.

Because of my mother's record-keeping, I can tell you that on September 30th, a feeding tube was inserted. I can also tell you that the day before, I started to get really agitated. It was as if I was fighting in my coma. This went on for two days, apparently. On October 1st I was found to have a liver infection. My eyes were jaundiced. I occasionally opened them while in the coma. I have no idea whether the agitation and the liver infection are in any way related. I can imagine how this affected my family.

I'm so melodramatic I think of Michael Jackson in the Thriller video opening his monster eyes and glaring at Ola Ray right before the famous dance sequence. I doubt it was that extreme but it still sounds scary.

I am sure I was medicated for the infection but a few days later, on October 4, the lines going into the left side of my body were infected, too. I developed a problem with my spleen. I'm not sure the exact cause but it raised serious medical concerns.
In fact, the doctor said that if I needed an operation to deal with this crisis, I wouldn't make it. Fortunately, the problem subsided and another crisis was averted.

I was a healthy, active coed before this accident. Now I'm lying lifeless in this bed in a medically induced coma! I may never walk again! Hell, I might not even survive this! But I wasn't drinking! This is so unfair!

It had been two weeks since the accident. I had hundreds of visitors, a vivid testimony to true love and support. I don't know whether there was any way I could sense the sheer outpouring of love. I obviously wasn't aware of my environment but there is part of me that feels I could sense the presence of all that love and that it helped me.

The days passed and the vigil continued. On October 7, I was back in surgery to operate again on my right wrist and my left arm.

On October 8, I stayed fairly passive, still sedated, still watched over by my army of worried visitors. One of my wrists slipped off the bone. It's hard to explain but my wrists was completely broke and metal rods held the two severed pieces together so they could heal.

On October 9, I woke up.

I knew I had been in an accident but I didn't realize how bad it was. In fact, in my comatose state I thought I had hurt my back. I am sure my back was hurting but I didn't realize how badly injured I was. My back felt stiff and I couldn't lift my head. Now thinking back, it was probably why I was fighting nurses and doctors and my arms were subsequently strapped down.

My first sensation was an awareness that my mother, both fathers, Uncle Gene and Uncle Kebby, were there at my bedside. I opened my eyes and looked around for the first time in almost three weeks. My family looked at me. I knew that there was something seriously wrong, although I wasn't feeling much pain.

I tried to sit up and my mother promptly pushed me back down into my pillows. I was ticked!
I looked around and saw that various machines in the room beeping were hooked up to me. To be honest, I felt fine.

Again, I was oblivious to the extent of my injuries. I didn't even realize I had that huge brace around my waist to protect my pelvis. One thing was immediately obvious, I couldn't talk, as I had a huge tube down my throat.

As I started to take it all in as my mother is trying to explain what happened to me, I realized that my feet were elevated on some sort of contraption that surrounded my lower legs in what looked like foam; actually it looked like Swiss cheese to me. Both my wrists were wrapped, with metal pins protruding from the sides of the right one. I then realized that there was a structure around my waist that stuck out about a foot all around with all sorts of pins and bars protruding from it.

It slowly dawned on me as my mom is explaining that I had not been in a minor accident the previous night, but I was very severely injured and I had probably been in the hospital much longer that I dared to consider. I became more and more grateful that I was still alive but I was very confused. It felt like a bad dream.

It was all a bit surreal. And to add to that feeling, my biological father was there, having flown in from Texas.

He is a minister and when he is praying he often speaks in tongues.

For those who are not aware of "speaking in tongues," it is one of the supernatural gifts of the Holy Spirit referred to in 1 Corinthians 12:4-10. Although, not exclusively, "speaking in tongues" is primarily practiced by Pentecostal Christians.

As it was apparent that my awareness had returned, my mother started to tell me all of my injuries. I so wanted her to stop. I wanted to say, "Ma, enough with the injuries. I feel fine," but, of course, I couldn't say a word. I just looked at her in stern consternation.

My family members were thrilled to see me awake but assumed I had the mind of a two-year-old. They talked to me very slowly, and looked very earnestly at me as they were speaking. I thought they were crazy! The more they treated me like this, the more agitated I must have become, because they proceeded to talk even more slowly and deliberately and it was driving me nuts! My brain may have been a little confused but it was working at my normal speed. Unfortunately, I had no way of conveying this to those slow-talking, Disney characters in my face but well-meaning people gathered around my bed. I was so frustrated!

I remember an old friend coming to see me and asking me "Tè do you know who I am? It's Monisa." I looked at her as if to say "Are you kidding me? Of course, I know who you are!" I could not for the life of me understand why my friends and family were acting like this.

It was so peculiar, like I was in *The Twilight Zone*. I either had them acting like I was practically a vegetable or in denial.

My cousin, Val, whose bridal shower we were celebrating on the day of the accident, thought I would still able to attend her wedding in a couple weeks. My mother had to explain to her, I absolutely would not be making her wedding, and further, I would not be reading the poem she anticipated me reading at the ceremony.

For me, the biggest disappointment was I wouldn't be attending Laila Ali's first professional fight in upstate New York with my boxing trainer, Ed. I guess I was suffering from a bit of denial myself because initially, I wasn't ruling it out. I wanted to meet Muhammad Ali! I couldn't communicate all these thoughts and questions in my head.

It wasn't until my sister, Simone, showed up that I could finally get someone to understand me. My sister and I are eight years apart and weren't particularly close but somehow, through some mysterious fraternal connection, she could read my grimaces, lips and every other facial gesture I could make enough to get the gist -- I was actually very alert.

Another solution to the communication problem was to use pen and paper. Unfortunately, I couldn't use either wrist because they were smashed but I could point to letters.

And so, a card with the letters of the alphabet on it was duly produced. The idea was that I could point to letters and spell out words. Great!

Now I could spell out whole words and sentences! There was one problem. I was doing this so fast that nobody could keep up! And no one thought to put a space bar in there, so they could distinguish between the words. I'll explain more about this later.

I was also frustrated because Simone could only stay in my room for about an hour a day because my nephew, Jeremiah, was only a little more than a month old. No babies or infants in ICU, although my Godson, Bobby was determined to get in to see me. This was one strong, determined young boy because they finally had to let him in. He wasn't even ten years old but he fought back tears and he told them "I want to see my godmother!" and so he did. His sister Phyre, my Goddaughter, was entirely too young to be allowed in.

A second alphabet card was introduced, with punctuation marks and gradually, the communication improved.

On October 12th, it was time for what became the infamous swallow test. This would determine whether I could have the feeding tube permanently removed. Since my awakening, the TV had been on and I was constantly exposed to food commercials!

The only taste I had in my mouth was the faint sensation of carotene, a bi-product of the cocktail given to me via the feeding tube. It drove me crazy! That awful taste in the back of my throat and the lemon mouth swabs that family rubbed on my lips to keep them from chapping were maddening. They were sweet and tart like a liquid Lemonheads candy.

Dr. Dan was the guy in charge of the swallow test and it helped that he looked a bit like George Clooney. I was so ready to go back to normal eating. I desperately wanted to gulp down the Pepsi and the hot microwave popcorn my mom had in her hand. This combo was often my mother's only meal for the day. After a few days of hearing the bubbles from the carbonation of the Pepsi and the smell of the hot buttered popcorn, I wanted my mother to eat it in the hall or somewhere out of my room. I was so frustrated that I could smell and practically taste food but couldn't eat it. Instead, I had to make do with a thick juice and a blue dye. Nothing else!

Fortunately my aunt, Elisa, my father's younger sister, who was not one to follower rules, snuck in some ice-chips. Thank God! But if my mother caught her, she knew she would be in trouble. My mother was like a hawk. Plus Lisa was only five years old when my mother & father got married so she's like her older sister. She didn't want to deal her wrath even now as an adult.

There was a bureaucratic screw-up and the test had to be repeated, which was hard to swallow--pun very much intended. So, a couple of days later, I had the test again. By now, my voice was returning and I was able to voice my displeasure about that "thick-ass juice!"

I was raised not to cuss and swear but I felt this situation gave me a certain leeway in that regard. I was pretty ornery, stuck in the bed, unable to move, completely constricted, with virtually no privacy and no control over my life. So I wanted real food no more thick-ass juice!

This test was to ensure I could swallow and liquids and food would go down my throat properly and not into my lungs then causing complications. One being Pneumonia. I may not have known the severity of all my injuries but I knew I was capable of swallowing properly. I've always felt in tune with my body. Moreover, people were talking to me as if I were a toddler and honestly there was nothing wrong with my brain.

My frustration and agitation manifested itself at night. While I was sleeping some weird creatures appeared to me. I called them "The little people". They looked like a mix of two creatures; rat monkeys. These were telling me nasty things.

"Nobody loves you!"

"These nurses are trying to hurt you!"

"Pull out your tubes!"

"Get out of the bed and walk. You can do it!"

If I did, I would have really hurt myself. They were truly tormenting. The only thing I could do was to pray to Jesus to remove them from my mind, even though, I perceived them to be right in my room – on my bed. They were real to me. It truly felt like a battle between good and evil. Apparently, this is not uncommon for a patient in my situation but that's irrelevant when you are being haunted in this way.

I felt very strongly about describing my tormentors to my family. I needed my aunts: Aunt Betty, Aunt Bon and Aunt Sandy to pray for me and specifically to rid me of these demons. One consequence of these terrors was that I dreaded going to sleep.
In fact, soon after I started being able to communicate through spelling on the alphabet card system, I started asking the nurses for a shot of B-e-n-a-d-r-y-l. One of my cousins said, "She's fine, only she would know how to spell Benadryl."

Correct spelling or not, I was so desperate for a peaceful sleep. The drug would typically help me sleep soundly until the very early hours of the morning and then I'd start to get agitated again.

When I woke up I was afraid. I was afraid that I would be left alone.

I was afraid that I wouldn't be with my family as the new millennium began and I would be at the mercy of some dark, mystical, cosmic forces that some were saying would manifest as we crossed into a new era. As a result, I would want to distract myself by watching TV. Typically, though, the remote control was both out of reach and impossible for me to pick up and operate.

I remember so vividly wanting that remote. How could it slip so far down the side of the bed that I couldn't reach it? I would try so hard, beads of sweat forming on my forehead, stretching my arm to find that remote. It's connected to the bed--it couldn't have fallen that far. It has to be under one of these sheets! Where is that remote! I felt so alone...so defeated. These little demons are winning! Where was my mother when I needed her?

My mom was actually at home getting much needed rest herself. Charmaine was a very tough South African nurse. Like most of the other nurses she practiced tough love with me and wouldn't cut me too much slack. I understand that they didn't want me to feel sorry for myself and I needed to do as much as possible on my own. Charmaine, specifically, told my mother to start taking care of herself and go home to get much needed breaks. I didn't like Charmaine.

There were some great nurses I encountered during my stay at Bridgeport Hospital, including Charmaine.

She was excellent at her job, I was a bit short-sighted then I'll admit. There was a gem of a nurse named Angel and he was. He assured me that one day I would forget all about this ordeal-it would be a faint memory. I didn't believe him but I appreciated him trying to comfort me. He said he had been in a horrific motorcycle accident years ago and found himself in a similar situation as me. He said it's just a memory now. I liked him a lot but unfortunately, he wasn't my nurse for long. I say that with a bittersweet tone because with the delightfulness of Angel came the rudeness of Frances.

Frances was on rotation for MICU. I will never forget her. She was so rude and boorish. As I write this now, her barbaric disposition is so vivid as if I'm back there in that hospital bed feeling helpless and subjected to her tyranny. I remember like it was yesterday that as she changed my bed and dressings, the name used for bandages that were soaked in saline then taped to my stomach, she would talk at me as if my situation was my fault.

I knew someday I would see her, hopefully in a dark alley. Seriously, I would just want to give her a tongue-lashing and let her know how off-putting and ineffective she was as a nurse. Further, she has no bedside manner and really no business being a nurse at all! As you can see, I feel just as strongly about this today as I did when I was laying in that hospital bed. Funny thing is I did see Frances years later.

We happened to be eating in the same restaurant and she appeared to be with her husband. I recognized her instantly and I'm talking some ten years later.

Some people have a wonderful, delightful effect on you and others bring about a revulsion or detestation that causes you to never forget them. Of course, Frances brought about the latter. I saw myself getting up from my table and walking over to give her a piece of my mind. You know how you see on television shows or in movies but then it switches back to reality and it's just your thoughts because you never really did it? That's what it was for me, a dream sequence. The reality is I was content. Not even Frances being in my presence could change my energy.

I thought about how happy I was and why would I let her change that even for a moment? She wasn't worth it. However, sometimes I do think I could have possibly helped another patient by letting her know the adverse impact she had on me and perhaps she would see the error of her ways but I somehow doubt it.

On October 19th I was moved out of MICU into a very small room. But it soon became apparent that this room simply could not accommodate all my visitors. As a result, I was moved to a much larger, more comfortable room that was much more like a suite. It was definitely an upgrade and I have to thank all of my many visitors who made it happen!

While in my spacious new corner suite, I started some primitive physical rehab. I'll explain the details of the move to the suite later. I was moved out of my bed into reclining wheelchairs. This was incredibly painful. My back muscles, which had done nothing for more than a month, now sprung painfully back to life. In fact, the pain was unbearable at times. This was the beginning of my rehab.

It was now late October and some other medical issues arose. The surgeons closed some of my stomach, which had remained open during this entire time. But it still remained slightly open and needed constant dressing.

Then one day one of the doctors, on my team of many, noticed a leakage on my pillow and lifted my head to discover I was bleeding. I thought it was a bedsore but it turned out this was an injury I didn't know about. I was familiar with bedsores because my Nana died from complications of bedsores that led to infection. She had Multiple Sclerosis and spent an excessive amount of time sedentary in bed or her wheelchair.

There was about a two to three-inch wound at the back of my head. I didn't know it at the time but hair would never grow there again. I would have to adapt. But in addition to this, I had something more serious than a bald spot.

If this manifested into an infection, I once again may not make it out of here alive.

With all these medical challenges I became an important stop on the medical students' rounds most mornings. The doctor would bring in a group of about a dozen students into my room. He would talk about me as if I didn't exist and then the students would just stare at me or some would purposely try not to make eye contact with me at all. Many of them looked uncomfortable, possibly at the thought that my horrific injuries could happen to them, possibly by their teacher's insensitivity. I was really annoyed. I didn't like the intrusion or being treated like a corpse. But, this is a teaching hospital and likely the reason why the doctors are young and innovative.

When I emerged from my coma and the doctor initially told me that I would be in the hospital possibly for six months and not walking in less than a year, I rolled my eyes at the thought of both. No, I would not be in this hospital bed in six months and I would be walking across the stage at my commencement ceremony to get my diploma. More importantly, my immediate goal was I was determined that I was going to be home and moving by Christmas and before New Year's Eve. And that was just nine weeks away.

FIVE

Love & Prayer

"Oh What Love" Vickie Winans

Oh what love
The Man had for me,
(Thank you, Jesus)
That He would give his life...
(Help me sing)

Oh what love
He has for me,
That He would give
His life...

My mother would listen to the Vickie Winans song, "Oh What Love", every day on her way to and from the hospital.

I survived my accident and horrific injuries and no matter how hard you try, it will be virtually impossible for you to prevent this fact from influencing your view about the severity of my situation. Cognitive psychologists call this "anchoring"; one piece of information sets your analysis of, and response to, the story. I didn't die, so while it was bad it wasn't that bad, is the normal reaction as your mind tries to measure the severity of the situation.

It was that bad. I could have easily died, or emerged with far worse lifelong injuries and disabilities than I did. That I didn't was, in large part, due to two factors, I believe. One was external and one internal was. One was love, the other, resilience.

During the first few cliff-hanging days and throughout my time in the ICU, while my life hung in the balance, I was showed so much love by my family and friends. There were definitely times where I sensed that love. As I mentioned earlier, being in a coma means you're non-responsive to stimuli not that you don't sense them.

First among my love support was, of course, my mother. My mother is an amazing woman. Strong, loving and principled, she taught me to be respectful and independent, curious and confident. Now, when I needed her the most, she was there every moment of the day. She marshaled my support, organized my visitors, kept them informed and kept me protected.

But, I don't want to overshadow how completely devastating this entire ordeal was for my mother. She had to live with the horrible reality that I might not survive this accident. Even after several days and numerous surgeries, I might die. She couldn't escape this possible reality. I thank God for family and friends that supported and prayed with my parents. Rev. Williams, my pastor at the time and other clergy were also very supportive.

Prayer works! Instead of being overtaken by the thought of me not surviving this ordeal, my mother journaled and prayed.

My mother kept a detailed journal of every surgery, doctor, nurse and visitor. I have a chronological timeline of every day I spent in the hospital. Can you imagine having the ability to do this while not knowing if your child will live or die? With the help of my friend, Tameeka, she sent *Thank You* letters to Stratford Emergency Responders and State Police-Troop G. She even dedicated a plaque to the nurses of SICU. I know this was her way of keeping herself busy while she waited for news from the doctors. My mother has always been one to make list and keep notes of everything. I am grateful she did this because it has been helpful for me in telling my story. In retrospect, she probably should be my co-author.

She also had the grim task of calling many of my relatives and friends when the accident happened and they all answered the call. There are many examples of the great response to my plight. I can't mention everyone in the text but I acknowledge them all at the end of the book in Remerciements (French for acknowledgments). I will share just a few examples.

My mother phoned one of my friends, more like a big sister, Jill. Jill and I met when she worked at the Women's Center at Southern. She had moved on from the university and was now working in

Chicago. When she got the call from my mother, she literally dropped everything and drove non-stop through the night to be at my bedside. I don't know many people who would put their lives on hold and drive non-stop to Connecticut from Chicago.

Dawn, a former director when I was working as a RA, was recently married. She was the Flo-Jo of the college: tall, beautiful and athletic. Her husband, Craig, was also an athlete and they made quite a couple. When Dawn heard about the accident she was instantly at my bedside, as well. In fact, she fainted at the sight of me. I hear I was a scary sight those first few days. Dawn was pregnant and my mother was concerned about her. My mom would've never let Dawn see me in such a state had she known she was pregnant. But Dawn wouldn't be deterred and visited regularly, sharing in the bedside vigil.

While I was working as a graduate intern, I had a fun director. Chris Piscatelli, otherwise known as "Pisci". Pisci was one of the leaders in Housing. He was like a big brother. You know the kind that rubs his knuckles in your hair after you've spent hours getting dolled-up? His way of showing love was to tease you and occasionally punch you in the shoulder. He used to tell me almost daily, "Hey Tè your mom called and said to bring her a pizza." He'd change the desired topping but he did this often and got a big kick out of it. I'm laughing now even writing about it. I can't explain it but it was funny every time.

When Pisci heard the news of my accident he raced to the hospital along with his best friend Denise. Denise was also one of the leaders of Residence Life at SCSU. The only problem was that initially, only immediate family members were allowed to visit. That didn't stop Pisci.

Despite the fact that he was very obviously a white Italian and our skins were quite different shades, he insisted that he was, in fact, my brother. The hospital staff was naturally cynical and hesitated to let him in to see me. My mother stepped forward and vouched for the fact that, indeed, Pisci was my brother. When the staff continued to hesitate he challenged them point blank, "Tell me I'm not her brother."

They let him in.

In some ways that incident stands as a metaphor for the lengths that my family and friends went to in order to support me and my mother. The President of the college also stepped up. We had our moments of disagreement as an undergraduate, as I was an activist. As a leader in the Black Student Union (BSU) we had planning meetings in my townhouse on campus about issues we had with the administration. We organized a class walk-out. President Adanti along with Assistant Dean Aaron Washington met us half-way on the SCSU Bridge. President Adanti coming outside to meet the students of the BSU half-way to discuss our issues was significant and earned my respect.

From that day forward, his door was open to me. He always lent me his ear and a cold Pepsi from his office fridge. We could always have a constructive dialogue and he would always ask me to participate in student-administration negotiations. In fact, I ran for local office -- as Alderman -- and he was very supportive of my political aspirations. We were very respectful of each other. He called my mother at the hospital to offer his support. Tragically, he himself was killed in a car accident while on vacation in Italy just a couple of years later. The new student center on campus is deservingly named after him.

Sadia was another friend from SCSU. We met at the Multicultural Center. We hit it off instantly and have been the best of friends ever since. Thinking back, I believe it is something about her being a "PK" from BK. Translation Preacher's Kid from Brooklyn, New York. She is authentic. You don't meet authentic people every day. Hopefully, you are blessed enough in life to encounter a few and when you do, you have the discernment to know it and cherish them.

Sadia was actually one of the first friends from the school to find out about my accident as it was clear that I had not returned to campus that fateful night. That reminds me, I later listened to my phone messages of all my friends on campus calling to see why I hadn't returned yet from home that weekend. It sounds like the intro of Mary J. Blige's "What's the 411" album.

Sadia was a few years younger than I and still very involved in her studies. But she was at my bedside every day. After a while, my mom got suspicious and asked her whether she was missing school to be at my bedside. Sadia admitted that indeed this was the case. My mom made sure she didn't do that anymore and made her promise she wouldn't skip any more classes.

Sadia also informed my mother that the entire campus was impacted by my accident and the BSU decided to cancel our annual trip to the New York Urban League Football Classic in New Jersey.
That year I was looking forward to the Battle of The Bands with Grambling University versus Hampton University. I later learned Hampton won the football game but I cannot imagine them triumphing over Grambling's band.

My cousin, Kellie, the one who had suggested we call off our nightclubbing and go home on the night of my accident, was seriously affected by my plight. In that irrational way that people do, because she had been with me the night of the accident, she felt some type of survivor guilt. She was definitely having a case of the "if onlys," running all sorts of scenarios in her head.

Since my accident, she hadn't been eating and was quite depressed. Of course, many people told her that she was being unnecessarily harsh on herself and the accident had absolutely nothing to do with her. But the human mind doesn't pay attention to reason.

Eventually, my mother took her aside and gave her a good lecture. I am sure my mother told Kellie that I would be devastated if I knew that she was blaming herself and that her reaction wasn't helping neither me nor her. She eventually lightened up or at least appeared to for the sake of my mother, but she was with me at every conceivable turn.

None of this was easy on my mother as strong as she is. My cousin, Val, was getting married in late October and I was slated to be a part of the ceremony. Val and my mom's lives were intertwined. She introduced my mom to my stepfather many years ago. My mom, six years older than Val, had always been like a big sister to her. When Val first heard about the accident she didn't appreciate the seriousness of it. With the wedding just a couple of weeks away, my mom told Val that I wouldn't be coming to her special event.

"What do you mean she's not going to be in my wedding?" said a stunned Val, failing to comprehend the fact that nobody was sure I was going to make it at all. Further, my mother couldn't promise she would be in attendance either given the situation.

When the wedding did come around, Val insisted that my mother leave my bedside for the first time for a few hours so she could attend. Val being the youngest of her brothers and the only girl was used to getting her way. And it appears my mother, being her "older sister" now aunt by marriage, perpetuated this as well.

Arrangements were made for her and my dad to attend the wedding. There were more than enough people willing to cover for her at the hospital. Of course, my mom insisted on giving complete instructions to her substitutes. Amongst these were instructions to a couple of my mother's chosen, trusted visitors, including Kellie, who were prone to be drawn in to my hysteria about the reality of "the little people" who were haunting me with their whispers and taunts.

"Don't argue with her!" my mom insisted as she left for the wedding.

The wedding was a much-needed break for my mother who soon had that South African nurse, Charmaine, on her case and making sure she took care of herself. Let me just say Charmaine was not your typical soft-spoken nurse with reassuring bedside manner. And her appearance was unassuming. She appeared to be Hispanic or maybe from the Virgin Islands. Her accent wasn't one you could easily identify so upon learning she was from South Africa, you were intrigued.

During my time in SICU, she was not my favorite. However, my mother loved her so I guess she couldn't have been that bad. I later learned she actually had her reasons for her demeanor.

"She's really going to need you when she gets through this. You need to take care of yourself," was Charmaine's message to my mother. She actually started making my mother leave the hospital to go home to sleep and spend time with my nephew. She warned her if she didn't get some rest and take care of herself, she wouldn't be in any shape to care for me when I got home. Further, ultimately I would be well and she would be sick.

The support for my mom took many forms. Of course, she wasn't going to work during the entire time of my convalescence. As it turned out, she was off work for six months. This would have created some serious financial problems for my mother if it hadn't been for some amazing support she got from another source.

The members of my mother's union donated sick days to her so she wouldn't lose her pay. Good thing my mom had been working for the City of West Haven for fifteen years already. Many contributed to, what in the end, must have been over 200 sick days. Not only that, there were other expenses that one wouldn't typically consider. One of these was parking.

Hospital parking was in a paid garage and with my mother almost constantly by my side, that parking bill was significant. No worries though. A sweet woman named Donna, from my mother's job, offered to cover her parking tab. It's the little things that really mean a lot.

Others helped, too. Toni Paine at the Credit Union helped my mom with some great advice to help minimize the financial impact. Officer Johnston also helped with insurance by trying to move along the completion of the police report. Many people either made food or arranged for it to be delivered. My mom worked at the West Haven City Hall in the same building as the police department. They always gave her an encouraging word and offered their support. To this day, they ask how I am doing.

My Southern University family showed their support as well. The members of my union donated sick days to me as well. The entire time I was out on sick leave for my accident, I never missed a paycheck. My staff of resident advisors (RAs) brought me cards they made along with my residents. At the time of the accident I was living with at least 200 students as the Hall Director for one of the largest residence halls on campus, Wilkinson Hall. At Southern we didn't call them dorms because dorms are where you sleep but residence halls are where you learn and grow. That is engrained in my head to this day.

Not only because it is true but because SCSU was my home away from home. I never lived anywhere longer than I lived on Southern's campus.

My uncles were a constant presence too. Uncle Gene made long trips from Atlanta. Uncle Kebby and my Uncle Mark were local and always around. In fact, Kebby worked with a Brazilian woman who knew Rodrigo and one day this woman showed Uncle Kebby an article in a Brazilian newspaper about the accident. Apart from that, however, there was no news from Brazil. Rodrigo's mom never did make contact with us.

All of this love and support for both me and my mother made a huge difference. People showed their love in different ways, but showing it any way was all that was needed. Some just showed up to keep vigil or contributed in other ways. My sister Shandra, we're just five months apart, decided to get me a gift. As she saw me lying helpless in my hospital bed, hooked up to drips and other equipment, she thought I could benefit from a gift. The next day she brought in a pair of diamond earrings and proudly put them on me.

The outpouring of love made a huge difference to me. That's the reason I was determined to honor everyone who supported me and my family with that tenth year reunion party, Carpè Diem.

By then I had survived and thrived but I didn't want anyone to forget or take for granted the effort they all put in during those difficult, dark times. They helped me get through those days, weeks, and months.

Fortunately, I had always been tough and I probably have my mom to thank for that, too. When I was growing up, my mom was strict and a stickler for following protocols and she still is even now that I'm grown…she provided order and structure that simply was not to be disobeyed. The only two times in my entire youth that I cut class, I was caught both times. I was taught to follow the rules and I expected others to do the same. As I grew older, I learned how to bend the rules a bit--you know the follow the spirit more than the letter of the law but never deviated from acceptable mores.

As an adult, I found joy in bending rules because it was, and is, so out of character for me. Even now, I still stay within certain boundaries. Without rules, we'd have anarchy! That has always been my thought. I need order and a certain level of normalcy. I'm a Capricorn, after all.

I always was a momma's girl. Thank God! My parents separated when I was young. To be honest, I may have started out as a daddy's girl but like giraffes, I had to adapt in order to survive. I mean my mom is all I had. Well not really, I had my Nana, Uncle Gene, my uncles and aunts but it was truly me & my mom.

Whatever my mother said was law. If she told me the sky was green and I went outside and found it was blue, I would still give her the benefit of the doubt because my mother was always right--when I was a child. "Perhaps it was green when she saw it last," I would reason to myself. This is in complete contrast to my little sister, Sìmone, who would respond to the same situation by asking "What is my mom talking about? The sky is blue!"

My mom also taught me the value of hard work and self-sufficiency. She is also a Capricorn. For example, when I was in the third grade, my mother got an additional job doing payroll on the third shift at Automatic Data Processing (ADP). Sometimes she had no choice but to take me with her and I wanted to go. Actually, I thought it was fun, especially when the food truck came by at 3 a.m. and served chilidogs. I liked her co-workers too. Imagine being a child hanging with adults on the third shift. I was still an only child then and always wanted to be with my mother. Aside from a few close cousins, I preferred the company of adults anyway. I have always been mature for my age and an old soul.

My mom was always challenging me. One day when I was four years old, we were driving home from some place. My mom stopped the car and asked me to give her directions on how to get home from where we were. I remember it was pouring raining. Sitting in the back seat, I proceeded to give her detailed directions for the route home.

Later, as a teen, she taught me other auto-related skills. She didn't teach how to drive though. She couldn't. Not because she was not able to but she just couldn't and I'll just leave it at that…

She taught me how to change a tire. Actually, she and Pops taught me how to change a tire. It was during my time as a novice driver that I got a flat. I called home and both my parents showed up. I smile thinking about it because that's the kind of support I had from my parents. They came together to bail me out of trouble.

So this became a teaching moment but this was no after-school special or NBC One to Grown on. It took no time before this became a competition between my mom and my dad on who knows how to change a tire best. They disagreed over the order of things. I quickly realized this may take a while. It was comical because they were both so committed. Nonetheless, I definitely know how to change a tire.

The tire debacle actually benefitted me a few years later when some college friends and I were on an excursion in a rental car in Atlanta. The tire blew and they were all resigned to missing out on the fun as we waited for the tow truck to come. No need to worry. I changed the tire as they watched in amazement and we were soon on our way in less than 30 minutes.

When I was seven, I traveled on an airplane by myself and by now, as a young woman, I was pretty independent and could adapt.

My mom gave me an undying faith in myself and I think it ultimately prevented me from dying.

I also had to adapt to a variety of schools. In Bridgeport, I transferred late fall from my school to a magnet school in the fifth grade, Park City Magnet. However, after my great-grandmother died we moved away and I went to another school. Fifth grade was tough as I was in no fewer than three schools.

Thompson was my new school in West Haven. I walked the two miles to school, which I actually enjoyed. There, my reading level was assessed as advanced and I was assigned literally a spot by myself in the corner of the classroom. I basically taught myself with little input from my teacher and got an A in advanced reading.

I felt very isolated there and many of the other kids didn't seem to like me because the teachers put me on this pedestal and labeled me this little genius. It was hard enough moving to a new town, new school and making new friends but to be labeled a little *Ms. Know-It-All* just made matters worse.

Kids couldn't wait for me to mess up. Every time I went to the blackboard to solve a math problem or read aloud, you could hear a pin drop. I believe this, coupled with other childhood occurrences, is why I am now self-reliant, a perfectionist and pretty good public speaker. I had to rid myself of stage fright early in life.

It wasn't all bad though. The friends I made were nice. We would have slumber parties and go roller skating at a roller rink in Orange near the movie theatre. My soundtrack at this time of my life was Motley Crue, Van Halen, Twisted Sister, Billy Idol and Billy Joel peppered with Michael Jackson and Menudo.

I then found myself as one of three black girls in Our Lady of Victory Catholic School. Thompson only went up to fifth grade so my only choices were either a parochial school or the local public middle school. The friends that I had made at Thompson were going to parochial schools and Our Lady of Victory seemed to be the best. I had a lot of friends there and did well.

The same year I started at Our Lady of Victory, the school adopted a Vietnamese family. The two boys of the family attended the school. I recall one of the first words they learned, along with certain four letter words, was *the N word*. Not only did they learn the word but also how to use it. Thanks to experiences such as this early in life, I faced adversity and bigotry at a young age. This has aided to my ability to be resilient later in life.

I remember being in religion class learning the prayers, Hail Mary and The Lord's Prayer, which I knew already. Strangely, I was challenged on whether I was Catholic or not. I knew being Baptist was under the Christian umbrella like Catholicism but wasn't quite able to fully articulate it then.

However, I knew asking me that question insinuating Black people aren't or can't be Catholic was off-putting. I knew *off-putting* even back then. I knew my Nana was Catholic so it was possible.

I knew even then that, even though, I was from Bridgeport, I was more evolved than these kids. I had already spent summers in LA and flew to the West Coast by myself. What did they know?

I must admit though, academically, I knew this was a good school. We had computers, went on nature trips to Nature's Classroom where we stayed in cabins for a week and we had civic responsibilities. We were expected to volunteer to help the elderly. Ironically, this was a catholic school with middle-class kids that lived in big houses with manicured lawns but they were mischievous and promiscuous. The girls were fresh and very advanced. The seventh graders were doing drugs before school on the playground while they appeared to be well-behaved, respectful students in their neatly pressed school uniforms.

The phys-ed teacher at Our Lady of Victory, Mr. Martha, looked like a real Ken doll. You know, Barbie's boyfriend. He was tanned year-round but anatomically correct. He assumed I was a natural athlete because I was from the inner-city of Bridgeport after all. I must be good at basketball and track. Wrong! I had Asthma! I was instantly on the girls' basketball team and track.

I wanted to be a cheerleader! I realized quickly a prerequisite was long blonde hair, which I did not have.

So, I played basketball but not well and ran track and was awful. No one trained me. The gun shot went off and I ran. I had no idea I was supposed to pace myself. He entered me in 100 meter event for the citywide catholic school games. This wouldn't be my last defeat on a track. Summers in Texas with my biological father would end similarly. What is this notion that I would make a great track star?
I want to be a cheerleader! I want the cute skirt and saddle shoes. I don't want to be an athlete...but I digress.

At the closing of my sixth grade school year, my mother decided to move back to Bridgeport. I was glad to leave. It was a nice community before West Haven became as developed as it is today. It's still a nice town but not as quiet as it was back then. Although, I would miss many of my friends in West Haven, in particular Markie, he and his father lived in our building. Markie's mother died in the Stratford Toll Booth accident. That was tragic.

It was the seventh grade and where would I go? On my own, I called the principal of the magnet school, Mrs. Hill, and asked whether I could come back. She found a place for me! Park City Magnet here I come...

My determination manifested itself in many situations. In high school, I so wanted to be a cheerleader. There was a problem however. I couldn't do a cartwheel, which was mandatory.

I even went to Polly's as a young girl but never could do a cartwheel. Polly's is a well-known gymnastics school in Stratford. My cousin, Kellie, who was on the squad, taught me everything she knew but even she was at a loss when it came to my cartwheeling ability or inability. It became a group effort.

Stacey, a gymnast that I remember watching do flips back when I was in elementary school was on the squad. We went to different magnet elementary schools but I recall seeing her flip. She was amazing because she wasn't one of those short, stocky little gymnasts. Stacey had bounce. She could do aerials and tucks so effortlessly. She was the squad's secret weapon.

Cheerleading is competitive after all. So, cheerleading tryouts...My friends, including my boyfriend, Terrance, watched with apprehension as I tried out for the cheerleading squad. They were more concerned than I was. When it came time, somehow, for the first time in my life, I actually did a cartwheel. I made the cheerleading squad. It also helped my score that I did a death-defying jump split during the tryouts that made everyone in the gym get chills. Terrance gasped as if he were in pain. Then he jumped and cheered as if I just competed in a gymnastics competition.

I had to thank Kellie, Stacey, Erin and Ebony for their help. Like I said, it was a group effort.

By high school I had developed confidence to stand up to anyone for what I believed in. This manifested itself on one famous occasion in tenth grade.

I have always been fascinated by chimpanzees and monkeys. I thought they were intelligent and underestimated and one day in my history class I expressed the opinion that at some point it will be shown that monkeys can communicate.

My teacher, Mr. Burns, encouraged the debate and soon took up the opposing position. As I started to get the upper hand, he began to prevaricate and stretch the facts as he was known to do. I called him out on it. I told him he shouldn't resort to making stuff up just because he was losing! This is a man who told students he commuted daily to work from Africa. I think he secretly found it humorous that high school students could actually be fooled into thinking he could commute from Africa.

I found it pathetic because he's the teacher -- the adult. Further, he wanted to be called Dr. Burns, yet at the time, he had not earned a doctoral degree. Even as a child, I couldn't condone such lies so, because he was a teacher, I showed him respect, I knew he was no match for me in a debate.

I earned a reputation for standing up for truth and advocating for the underdog. My high school administrator, Mr. Karcich, would always say to me as I scurried behind him trying to keep up with his pace, "Hanks, you should go to law school and be a lawyer because you're always arguing someone else's case." Mr. Karcich was a tall man, standing at about 6'7". I was always pleading a classmate's case to him or arguing against some form of social injustice I felt we as students were being subjected to.

I felt uncomfortable if I didn't challenge unfairness. In graduate school, I was afforded the opportunity to respond to my third grade teacher, Ms. Davidson. She was mean and jumped to horrible conclusions. One time, a friend of mine and I happened to get the same score on a quiz. She assumed wrongly that we were collaborating (i.e. cheating) and punished us even after we took the quiz a second time while she watched us like a hawk and got the same score. She still punished us by eliminating recess and making us eat lunch in the classroom with her.

The meal was the cafeteria's version of a McDonald's Filet o' Fish. I asked for a packet of relish and mayo. After I mixed them together as I had seen my mom do, I proudly announced, "Look Ms. Davidson, I made tartar sauce!" Ms. Davidson responds, "Eat your lunch Shantè and stop playing with your food!" was her tart reply. I was devastated and embarrassed.

I knew I was correct in making tartar sauce and surely this woman was mistaken because I would never play with my food. That would be improper and I never conducted myself in an improper manner.

Although, I was disappointed by her ignorance of the ingredients in tartar sauce, because I respected teachers as an authority, I simply sat there quietly and ate my food. Most importantly, I couldn't let her see my disappointment because after all, I knew I was right. So I took my spork and smeared my homemade tartar sauce across my sandwich and ate it.

So, some fifteen years later while in grad school, learning about teaching creatively. The professor challenges us to think of a teacher in our past who was a "creativity killer". He encouraged us to write to him or her, explaining why we thought their techniques were wrong and give an example of how they killed our creativity.

I duly wrote the letter to Mrs. Davidson, who I discovered was still teaching at the same school. I expressed the hope that "you haven't killed the creativity of other students." I strongly suspect she had.

I have always been independent and viewed needing support as a sign of weakness. Even though, I am always willing to help others, I rarely ask for help myself. I now know this is wrong but I can't help it. It's one of those things.

As I get older I have loosened up a little and now will challenge some rules rather than blindly accept them. But my mother helped me to realize that there was nothing I couldn't do -- and do it on my own.

Two mantras my mother taught me still ring in my ears, "Can't means not able and you are able to do anything." The other is "You were not born a twin so you can do anything by yourself." Thus why I'm self-reliant and whenever faced with a challenge I will try to move mountains to overcome it.

When I first recovered consciousness, the doctors talked to me and told me that my recovery would take a long time; six months in the hospital and maybe a year before I could walk. Six months! A year! No way!

They didn't know who they were talking to. I simply rolled my eyes because, of course, I couldn't talk; I was trached. It was all I could do so I tried to roll them as hard as possible and hoped they communicated exactly what I was thinking to the doctors and my mother.

SIX

Rehabilitation

*Apparently there is nothing
that cannot happen today.*
- Mark Twain

It took me a few days after I emerged from my coma to really grasp the nature of my injuries. The full realization of my physical condition was hampered by medicine that numbed me and the fact that pretty much everything was being done for me. I was in the hands of doctors and nurses, and after that, my mother. As the sobering reality dawned on me, I wanted to regain as much control of my world as possible.

I have been told I am a controlling person so you can imagine how difficult it was to be powerless. Although, I quickly learned just because I was not in total control of my body physically, I was still in control and, even though, I had an amazing team of doctors, God had the final say. However, at the time, I felt helpless but still very stubborn. I eventually, learned how to channel this. That was difficult while I still needed surgeries for vital functions but now, after a month in SICU, I was stabilized enough to be transferred out of the Surgical Intensive Care.

The move out of SICU was a big step forward, even if I was a long way from actually taking any physical steps at all and it was literally one room over.

I sped through this experience a few chapters ago. I need you to fully grasp what was happening at this time. This was considered a step forward because I no longer had nurses assigned to just me. This next level, called Medical Intensive Care Unit (MICU), allowed two patients assigned to these set of nurses. I also could start my recovery or so I thought.

The first order of business is removing this trachea so I could talk. Me not talking is like your heart not pumping blood. It's what I do. It is imperative to survive. To this point, as I told you I was spelling my conversations. Because only Sìmone could read my lips, I would only communicate freely about an hour a day. My nephew, Jeremiah was only a little over a month old and could not come into ICU. When Sìmone would come into my room, another family member had to watch him in the waiting room. I was later told that every time they would wheel me down the hall for one of my many surgeries he would let out a loud cry to make his presence known to me.

I often reflect on how, although Sìmone and I are eight and half years apart and in my opinion we practically had two different childhoods, we had a sibling connection when it counted.

I would find solace in that one hour every day that I could talk freely, even though, there was no sound, she was my voice. She would effortlessly read my lips.

One of my cousins came up with the idea of writing out the alphabet on a big gold envelope to see if I could spell what I needed to say. This idea was after unsuccessful attempts to get me to write out my thoughts. Unfortunately, my wrists were both broken in the accident so I had metal rods holding them together and bandages wrapped around them. My fingers were too numb and bandaged to hold any writing utensil.

Someone suggested the magnetic letters on a board like preschoolers play with when they're learning the alphabet. But again, I couldn't pick up the letters to place them on the board. So the idea of my pointing at the letters as a way to spell out my thoughts worked---at least for me.

My family was skeptical because they weren't sure if I had my full mental capacity. I guess rolling my eyes at the doctors didn't convey to them that I was *Shantè*. I never had a poker face so you would think that my frowns, nostril flares and eye communication would have been enough but I guess not. I had been in a medically induced coma for weeks and the doctors warned my parents I may not come back with my full capacity. It was waiting game. They told them to be prepared, she may come back as herself or with the mind of a toddler.

Aside from the medication, I was myself. They realized this quickly because I was spelling sentences, paragraphs and entire conversations because I could finally communicate. I had questions, comments and demands. And when I was frustrated, I didn't want to be bothered at all.

Remember I told you, my friends and family were also surprised I remembered them. I don't know if I was expected to have amnesia. I did not remember the details of the accident but I remembered my life and the people in it. I remembered thinking I'm the one in this bed why are you all acting like you have head injuries? Even my mom was speaking slowly and very close. I don't like close talkers or slow talkers. I'm near-sided but prefer a certain distance and think fast so if I could, I would've been snapping my numb fingers to speed it up!

I previously mentioned that after ICU, I was moved into a small, standard size room on a different ward. My move into a small room had some advantages. Because I was no longer in ICU my visitor list wasn't restricted to family members and those who could successfully fake being family members. This more open access actually got me thinking about the people I hadn't seen, heard or sensed -- people I hoped would have visited me but apparently had not.

My cousin, Robert, had transferred to Southern and, despite the fact that he is a few years younger, we hung out a lot together. He was a like a brother to me. He took my accident hard. He volunteered his organs and blood. I can't write this without giggling because we are tough until something happens to someone we love, then we are all mushy and emotional.

I know he would have given me anything that I needed. However, coming to see me was apparently too hard for him. Maybe he couldn't come to the hospital in part because he had just seen his dad finally succumb to a long battle with cancer a few years back.

Hospitals aren't typically fun places and they are often associated with very sad times in people's lives. There was another good friend of mine, whom I was very aware had not been at the hospital, but she had other motives. More about that later…

But I will tell you about one very good friend that I noticed had not been around. Later, it was explained to me that she was going through a divorce and her therapist told her because she was dealing with too much stress (her sick friend and her marriage unraveling) She would need to choose and deal with one at a time. She chose to deal with her divorce.

Another advantage to moving into a regular hospital room was that I was no longer restricted to hospital food, or to put it another way, it was easier for me to develop an alternative meal plan.

I had lots of requests. I remember Val bringing me lime sherbet, Kellie bringing me her mom, my Aunt Karen's homemade Iced Tea. Both my Aunts Karen and Rene make an awesome fresh-brewed sweet iced-tea. My cravings were through the roof! It had been so many weeks that I was fed intravenously. Now I wanted food! One night Sìmone came up and told me to taste something that I had never heard of but she was convinced I'd like it. It was Taco Bell's newest item; the Chalupa. She was right.

Although, I was out of ICU, I still required surgeries on my fractured bones. I recall one occasion when I was being prepped for surgery two young anesthesiologists, a male and a female, came into my room to insert an IV port into my arm in anticipation of surgery early the next morning.

By this time, I had undergone several surgeries and combined with my notoriously small veins, this meant that finding a suitable vein was becoming problematic. My arms seemed like worn-out pin cushions. The two doctors were searching up and down both my arms looking for a suitable spot for the IV port, even as my room was full of visitors.
So, while I'm talking with my relatives, my veins were being explored, prodded, poked, invaded and generally abused by the anesthesiologists.

The room suddenly seemed very small and in truth it wasn't big enough to accommodate all my visitors. In the end, after considerable exploration, the two doctors gave up. Their solution was to insert the IV into my jugular, once I was in the OR and knocked out by enough medication.

One of my attending nurses was a delightful young West Indian girl. She liked to wear the more traditional nurses clothing, the sort of outfit you might find in a movie of yesteryear. Actually, it was just like the nurse outfit the woman wore on the cover of Life Magazine with the sailor kissing her in Time Square after returning home in 1945. She was compassionate and could see that the room was too small for me and my entourage, especially when my veins were being assaulted. I'm not sure exactly what she did but not too long after the anesthesiologist's incident, I was informed I was going to be moved.

When the time came, I was duly transported into a room that was on the corner of the floor. In fact, it wasn't so much a room as it was a suite! It must have been 600 square feet with a separate area for the living room and TV. I felt like a celebrity! In truth, being in that room made me feel as if I was regaining a little control of my life. Up until now, I felt as if my life had been controlled by doctors and nurses but I was beginning to feel more normal.

The suite was a bonus that certainly helped my
recovering spirits but, of course, I still had a very
long way to go. However, there was soon talk about
my transfer to some sort of rehabilitation facility.
There was a place called Gaylord in Wallingford
but the concern was that because of the large brace
around my waist, I wasn't quite ready to head there.
The other alternative was Mediplex, a convalescent
home in Milford about twenty minutes from my
home.

I never heard of Mediplex but was familiar with
convalescent homes because Nana had been in one
after a rapid decline in her Multiple Sclerosis. It
seemed like an odd place for me to be going,
though. It was mainly for much older patients and I
would surely stick out being that I was a young coed in my prime. However, I still needed a fair
degree of medical attention -- medication
management and regular attention to my numerous
bandages, especially around my still open stomach.

I was duly transferred to Mediplex. I distinctly
remember rolling through the lobby in my hospital
bed on my arrival. Many of the staff lined the way,
looking very solemnly at me. Perhaps they could
identify with me in some way. I was certainly about
their age and I guess they might have been thinking
that it could easily be them with a crushed body.
I suspect they could identify with me a whole lot
more than they could with their typical patient, an
elderly man or women with a terminal condition
and some with diminished mental capacities.

The move out of the hospital was liberating. At Mediplex I had much less of a sense that my life was being controlled by the medical professions. The nurses seemed to enjoy attending to my needs and chatting with me. I became quite close with some of them. In fact, many of the nurses used to hang out in my room. I would let them watch soaps with me on their breaks. Although, I was very particular. If I could smell that you had been smoking cigarettes, you couldn't stay in my room. My senses were so sharp! I recall telling one CNA I could smell the bacon, egg and cheese breakfast sandwich she had eaten on her breath. The nurses and nurses aids got a kick out of me because, although I was bedridden, I was sharp.

The one doctor who did venture into my room, however, was always unwelcomed. One day, when I was lying comfortably in bed watching a soap opera on TV, a man entered my room and introduced himself. He was a psychiatrist. He was there, no doubt, to assess me but the fact is I didn't want to be assessed. I finally could grasp the television remote with my hand and control the TV.

When I was in the hospital I struggled many late nights trying to hold the remote but my fingers were too numb and once it slipped out, it would be lost down the side of my bed. Even though, I was their only patient nurses would get tired of coming to hand it back to me. They were so mean.

Every night when my mom would leave to go home to rest, she would be sure to leave the remote in my hand. I fought every night with the remote and those little people...

The psychiatrist tried to engage me in conversation but he wasn't very engaging. The TV was a lot more interesting. Did I mention I had cable too? He sat in a chair asking me questions to which I gave very short answers. When he wasn't getting much out of me he turned and talked to my mother as if I wasn't there.

"She needs to talk about the accident," he said. I do? Why?

"She might not be able to drive again." What? He doesn't know who he is talking about. At each visit, I got more and more irritated.

At his next visit he asked me whether I was angry. I said, "yes." He asked "what makes you angry?" I said "you -- you and all your questions interrupting my time watching my shows." I was angry.
I felt like this psychiatrist was taking away the little bit of control I finally had. I was not willing to go backwards.

When he left I told my mother that I really didn't want to see him again, and I didn't.

I understand that some people might need counseling after a horrific accident but, honestly, I didn't think I did. I am not a person to dwell on the past. I was looking towards the future. And besides, I had my own strategies to help me through difficult times. I was just eager to get this metal contraption off my waist so I could walk out of this convalescent home and get back to my life.

As for my fears, I had developed the ability to close my eyes and go to a safe, relaxing place. This was a type of guided meditation that is used by some therapists and it certainly worked for me. It was not difficult for me to close my eyes and take myself back to 41 Lewis Street, the home of my maternal grandparents, Pop & Nana's house. In my younger years, it was heaven, a secure and loving haven.

I could still take myself there, even though, the passage of time ultimately changed the meaning of the place for me. It was the place where my grandmother first learned about her having Multiple Sclerosis. It was a place that was associated with my grandfather, who in the early years had been loving and supportive but this later changed. Adults always tell you there's more to a story but you're too young to understand. I've always been pretty cut & dry, black & white about things though. I have my thoughts and opinion on how and why things changed within the family.

The turn of events that happened later hasn't stymied my memories of childhood growing up as the oldest grandchild and my loving being at Pop & Nana's house with their dog, Cherokee. He was my dog as far as I was concerned. Cherokee was a mild tempered German Shepherd. The only dog I grew up around as a child. Later, they brought home some little pup named Lady but I never warmed up to her. She wasn't even a Cherokee lookalike. She was a poodle.

Unfortunately, 41 Lewis Street will always have to be a fond memory. The home itself was later acquired by Park City Hospital on the grounds of eminent domain, as they needed the street for their parking lot. The house no longer exists. One of my life's fondest memories is a true life Joni Mitchell song...*Don't it always seem to go that you don't know what you've got till it's gone. They paved paradise and put up a parking lot.*

Despite those realities, however, I still visualized that home as an entirely peaceful sanctuary and when I meditated about it, my soul was calmed.

If my soul was calmed sometimes my body wasn't. I remember vividly one Friday night I was given Percocet after a physical therapy session. I hadn't started walking yet but we started exercising my legs with light weights. Because I hadn't used my legs in months, the slightest workout seemed overwhelming. Later that evening I was a bit sore.

Apparently, I am allergic to Percocet. I began to itch as if little insects were crawling all over my body. I couldn't reach all the parts of my body that was itching and I started getting hot. I was feeling insects and suffering from heat flashes all at once.

My mother and friend, Tawanda, were there telling me there's no insects. It didn't matter, I was convinced. They had to call in a nurse to give me a sponge bath in order to calm me.

This was not a typical Friday night at Mediplex. I typically looked forward to Fridays because Tawanda would bring movies, take-out and stay the night. Her husband would watch the kids so she could stay overnight with me. It was like a slumber party. It provided some normalcy and a needed reminder that I was getting my life back.

My cousin, Robert, who couldn't bring himself to visit me in the hospital, finally showed up at the convalescent home expecting to find me in better spirits. Unfortunately, when he walked into my room, I was throwing up and in such pain, that I was about to be transferred to the hospital for emergency care.

Generally, however, I was in much better shape and in more control. You would be surprised to know that when you can't walk, your body doesn't function properly. Walking keeps you regular. If you are not regular, you become impacted.

If you do not move your bowels, you will need surgery to remove all of that waste from your intestines or you will become toxic. Brings new meaning to being full of it! I've never been accused of being full of shit but it is medically possible.

I was rushed to the hospital that day and luckily they were able to give me a much more effective laxative that allowed me to move my bowels. Surgery averted and I could return to Mediplex. I was better but I don't recall seeing Robert for quite some time after that. Now that I think about it, I don't think I saw Robert again until I went home.

I also received other visitors who, for one reason or another, had not visited me while I was in the hospital. One of these was a good friend of mine -- or so I thought. Well, actually she visited me at the hospital but not after I regained consciousness. By then she had gotten what she came for.

This buddy of mine resurfaced at Mediplex. She happened to mention that she had spent some time with two friends of mine -- they were brothers. I was very attached to the oldest brother, we had a special relationship but I thought this girl might enjoy the other brother's company.

As she told me her account of a trip with these two guys to a Knicks game, it became clearer to me that it wasn't the younger brother she had been hanging out with but with the oldest, my guy.

After she admitted that they had ended the night back in her apartment and "*all we did was kiss*," she felt the need to defend herself.

"We were so distressed at your situation, we were consoling each other. We thought you were going to die," she added, as if this was meant to make me feel better.

What she didn't realize is I had a conversation with my guy, now demoted to "the guy" prior to her coming to visit to explain after she got off work that day and he told me the name of the movie they went to see. Conversely, she told me the name of a different movie so in essence they went on two different movie dates and possibly a Knicks basketball game all while in distress over me possibly dying. At least this is what I am supposed to believe.

"Let me get this straight," I said, "You thought I was going to die so to console yourself you hooked up with a guy I really like?"

Before she could answer, I asked her to leave. I was so upset that my mom was concerned that the incident had seriously affected me. She called the two of them and warned them that if this incident set me back in any way, she would be very, very upset with them. All my friends respected "*Robin*". We call our mother's by their first names when they're not in our presence--our stab at defiance.

I knew the incident wouldn't set me back. Even though, this guy and I were very close or so I thought and he's very close to my family so I knew he would still be in my life in some uncomfortable way. I had much more important things on my mind though, like getting back on my feet. Besides, after what happened on Thanksgiving, I was focused because I had to be out of there before Christmas. This was my secret plan that I hadn't shared with anyone else.

Thanksgiving…Thanksgiving was an absolute disaster! My mom and family had a plan to make me feel as if I was really at home. She reserved a meeting room in the convalescent home and decided we would celebrate Thanksgiving together as family in our traditional way. My mother brought the china from home and made her usual Thanksgiving feast. She was determined to make me feel as much at home as I could without actually being there. And this year we had a lot to be thankful for.

Of course, my mother executed the plan to perfection. The room was converted into our home away from home. My family members were there and we were all ready for a great celebration. I was going to sit at the dining table and feel at one with my family finally!

Shortly after entering the room, just prior to pulling up to the table for dinner, I had to go the bathroom, which was always an ordeal.

The nurses took care of me, calmed me down and then wheeled me back down to the conference room where my family was waiting. Then it happened.

I had envisioned sitting at the table, eating off our traditional settings and feeling connected to my family. However, when I was wheeled up to the table, it was clear that my vision was not going to be realized.

I had a reclining wheelchair and this meant I couldn't get myself positioned to the table at all. This chair was a monstrous contraption reminiscent of Hannibal Lecter's chair in the movie Silence of the Lambs. Whichever angle the chair was turned, there was no way I could reach the table. I cried so hard. So much of my expectation and the reason for my mom's effort was that I would be able to physically sit at the table.

My presence at the table had great symbolic meaning and it had driven us to plan and execute this vision. But it just wasn't going to happen like that.

I ended up eating off a tray that was positioned on top of my wheelchair and I sat close to the table but surely not at the table. It was great to be with my family but part of me was very upset.

I stewed over the experience the entire weekend. When Monday came I called my orthopedic surgeon, Dr. Langeland, and asked to talk to him immediately. I had made up my mind -- I didn't want a repeat of Thanksgiving. I wanted to be home by Christmas.

Dr. Langeland told me the brace would need to be on ideally for ten to twelve weeks, which meant, theoretically, it could be removed on December 27th. That would be followed by several weeks of rehab, until I could move under my own power again. I negotiated with the doctor. Remove the brace the eleventh week and that would give me almost two weeks to learn to walk again. Then, I could be home by Christmas. He bought into the plan.

I was determined. And one thing that I was really determined about was that neither my mother nor any of my family would know my plan until it was time to leave Mediplex, which I hoped I could do on or before Christmas Eve.

December 24th is a big day in our family. We gather at my Aunt Sandy's house, have a festive meal, and sing Christmas carols which includes a competitive Shepard Family Rendition of *The Twelve Days of Christmas*. I was determined to be there.

Amy was the person in charge of my rehabilitation. She made it her job to get me literally back on my feet. God Bless her!

When I told her my plan she bought into it, too. Amy worked at Mediplex part-time but because we were the same age, she felt a connection and promised to work with me extra time in the evenings and weekends to give me every chance of realizing my ambitious goal.

I had the surgery to remove my brace on December 14th. What a relief! Or was it? When I got back into my bed after the surgery, I couldn't even sit up. My back muscles were so weak they couldn't support me. It was the strangest feeling having no control over my body. I thought I must be in a dream or maybe it was the meds from surgery. Then I realized I was awake and alert so it must be the bed. That must be it! One of the nurses must have changed the angle of the bed.

No one had changed the angle of the bed nor was I dreaming. I was just coming to terms with muscles that had been asleep for ages and a body that was going to have to learn how to balance and move itself. Muscular atrophy set in my young previously active body.

It seemed just a short time ago I was in the Southern gym lifting weights with the summer conference assistants paint crew. We worked out almost every day. The motto that summer was "Get Physically Fit". Now I can't even control my back muscles to sit upright. I just kept falling over like an infant.

I also had another challenge. I needed my mother to be out of the facility while I was working with Amy, so she would have no idea of my plan. She knew that I was coming home for Christmas Day but assumed I would be returning to the convalescent home the next day to continue my rehabilitation.

My mother loves to shop for Christmas gifts and, of course, I was in no position to go shopping. I gave her an almost endless list of gifts to buy for family members. While she was out shopping, Amy and I got to work.

On December 15, the day after the surgery for the removal of my brace, I was wheeled down to the rehab center. My aunt, Elisa, the only family member who was privy to my little secret, came to visit and help me take my first steps. I was helped out of my wheelchair and stood between two parallel bars, which would support me as I took my first steps in over three months.

I clung to the bars as I readied myself to walk again. My mind so desperately wanted to walk. However, my legs didn't seem to get the message.
My legs were itching horribly and a burning sensation relentlessly shot through them. I stood there willing my right foot to move, but it just wouldn't. It felt as if my feet were disconnected from the rest of me. Suddenly, it occurred to me that this wasn't going to be as easy as I thought it would be.

My aunt tried to be supportive and encouraging but my feet couldn't move! My thick, muscular legs that had previously sustained cartwheels, splits, dancing and soccer now were not even strong enough take a step.

Amy explained to me that my muscles in my legs simply hadn't been used in a long time and it was going to take a while to get them operational again. Atrophy had set in and I was going to have to put in the work to walk again. She encouraged and cajoled me as my aunt cheered me on. I was determined. I waited months for this day. Eventually, my foot moved ever so slightly forward. It was *One Very Small Step for Man, but a Huge Leap for Me*.

It seemed like ages before my left foot could move at all but eventually it, too, moved a small distance. But my balance was non-existent and I felt I was going to fall over at any moment. I was sweating and breathing heavily and my whole body hurt. I felt defeated. Somehow, however, I managed to repeat these tiny steps twice more before I decided that was enough for today. Amy and my aunt told me I did well but I felt defeated.

When I got back to my room and was helped into bed, I was so upset. I had made a huge effort and had barely moved. I cried and cried. Then, thankfully, I fell fast asleep. I was exhausted! Those 6 steps felt like a total body work out - a marathon. I must've slept until after nine that night.

I didn't want to worry my mother so I just told her it was tough but I'll try again tomorrow.

The next day, with mom again out Christmas shopping, I was down in rehab with Amy. My legs still were incredibly painful and slow to respond to my will, but they moved a little further than the day before. Later, Amy came back and we started "walking" the hallways. Step by painful step, I recovered my balance. For the next few days Amy supported me and guided along the hallways and even into the stairwells. Soon, I had graduated to a walker but after each jaunt my legs and back were excruciatingly painful. It felt like I had severe and constant charley horses. Amy worked on my sore legs and on my spirit.

The effort and the pain did start to pay off in handsome ways. For one thing, I could now go to the bathroom by myself. Yes, I could actually use a real bathroom without any assistance! I could put on clothes! The intense pain and the frustration were worth it.

Then there was the day I got an unexpected visit.
My *Aunt Flow* showed up surprisingly. I hadn't noticed that I had not gotten my period for the past few months. Probably because I had so many other more pressing issues but my mother did. In fact, she was happy to hear Aunt Flow made an appearance.

She had previous discussions with my doctors regarding my ability to have children after all the physical trauma my body suffered from the accident.

The idea that shortly after the pelvic bar was removed that my cycle started showed signs of my body being normal again and hope. The idea of children or the inability to have them hadn't crossed my mind to this point. Good thing my mother was on top of that.

After ten days of extreme pain, and workouts, it was almost time for me to go home. I had achieved my goal. I was now walking with a walker and occasionally with the 3-prong cane. We tried crutches – well I tried to appease Amy but I knew they wouldn't work.

While I was doing my therapy I was also scheduling hair appointments and getting used to wearing clothes again. With all the strides we've made in modern medicine, there have not been any upgrades to the Johnny Coat. My mother did buy me a few moo moos. Never thought I would be classifying a moo moo as a fashion upgrade but they were.

I was now wearing sweatpants, t-shirts and sneakers. I felt much better when visitors came to see me. I was sitting upright and clothed. Even though, I had come a long way, I looked very different sitting in the wheelchair in the convalescent home.

I hadn't noticed but for all these months, I hadn't seen myself in a mirror. I could tell from my fingers that I lost weight but didn't realize no one showed me a mirror all this time.

It was now Dec 20th, when my mother arrived after holiday shopping, Amy and I talked with her. We explained to her that I would be going home Dec 23rd. My mother says, "We knew she would be coming home for Christmas and we would bring her back Dec 26th."
Amy explains, "No, she will not be returning. Her bed will no longer be available. After a patient stays out 24 hours their bed goes to the next person on the waiting list."

Amy gave my mother a list of things she would need to get done over the next 3 days in order to prepare the house and the family for my arrival. She would need to get medical supplies and set up the bathroom so I could use it, schedule appointments with nurses, physical and occupational therapists. My mom looked confused. Why did she need to do all that, after all I would only be home for a day?

It took a few minutes for her to realize what Amy was saying. It had not occurred to her that I was really coming home for good. The nightmare that we had been living for the past few months was almost over. It was almost too good to be true.

When Amy told her that I was, in fact, going home for good my mom was shocked, then nervous. Then incredibly excited! Her long hospital and convalescent home vigil was over. For three months she had been by my bedside every hour of the day and night. Now I was coming home! Under my own power...well sort of. No more daily Heparin shots in my thigh! Not that I felt them anyway. My thigh was numb thanks to my broken femur.

I made it to Aunt Sandy's on Christmas Eve. I wore a brand new gray DKNY outfit with my NIKE Air Max and was able to navigate up the front steps of my aunt's house. No one was expecting me to be there and certainly not moving under my own power. In fact, when I walked in and sat next to Gram my family didn't immediately register that it was me. They simply were not expecting me. Then it was like, *Oh my gosh*! It's you!

The younger cousins were in the basement and they came up to see what all the fuss was about. We hugged, we kissed and they cried. They complimented me on how good I looked because they had not seen me standing upright for a while. They could now see I was about forty pounds lighter but this was a weight loss journey that I would not recommend.

We sang our traditional carols, competing in various groups and having a lot of fun. It was great to be home but I knew it was also the next step of my journey.

This was truly a Christmas Miracle! Christmas this year was especially magical. I was home! I felt like a child again because everyone came to visit and bought me gifts.

SEVEN

The Road Back

*Healing is a matter of time, but it is sometimes also
a matter of opportunity.*
- Hippocrates

Being home for Christmas and to bring in the New Year was amazing! It being the end of the millennium and the start of a new era made it all the more wondrous. Rather like me, despite predictions of doom, the New Year showed itself to be resilient and predictable. All the customary celebrations occurred and the world did not end. I was out there celebrating, too. Well out of the hospital but I spent New Year's Eve at home with family and friends.

Everyone came to my house to celebrate with me. We celebrated the same way we would have had we gone out. We even danced in the kitchen. Undeterred by my immobility, I was up balancing, trying to keep moving in synchrony with the music. No matter what is going on, I always feel better when I'm dancing.

If the world was going into a new chapter in its history on January 1st, 2000, so was I. I wanted to leave the horrors of my accident behind but to do that, I had to complete my rehabilitation and resume my life.

But life was never going to be quite the same. Unbelievable how life can change in just six minutes.

Over the holidays, many friends and relatives came to visit me at the house. If there was cause for celebration I was at the center of it. Not only did I have reason to be thankful and grateful, my visitors did too, and they showered me with love and more gifts than I had ever received at Christmas time. It was a very loving time.

Despite familiarity, friendship and family ties, several people seemed to relate to me differently now that I had come back from the precipice of death. It was as if my recovery from so close to death signaled that I had special powers and cosmic connections. This was to be one of the hallmarks of my recovery but in the last week of 1999 I was still trying hard to regain my balance and my life.

When the festivities and holidays were over, and my friends had returned to school and resumed their lives, I was back to the hard, unglamorous and distinctly arduous task of relearning some basic skills. My cousin, Deja, had been giving me a lot of help with the small necessities of life, like getting out of a chair and stepping into the shower but with her departure back to school, I was left more to my own devices.

My mother, of course, was still at home full time, overseeing my recovery and running me around to places, notably, the rehabilitation center. If not her, then Simone was my chauffeur. I really missed driving.

Occupational therapists also made house calls and frankly, their visits drove me insane. Not literally of course, but it seemed so mundane to play with my hands, fingers and wrists. They wanted to carry on what I considered mindless conversation and I often felt obligated to entertain them. It was not their fault that I rarely wanted to be bothered. They were doing their job. I was just tired of sitting there waiting for the next medical professional to show up and either ask me how I'm doing, poke & jab me for blood or as I call it, talk me to death.

The therapists came to my house twice a week and were working on my wrists and movement generally. They wanted me to develop dexterity in my hands by giving me games to play with my fingers. I understand what they were trying to do but playing finger games wasn't a high priority for me. I would rather sew or do something creative.

My mother bought me a sewing machine for Christmas. I spent a lot of the winter months making clothes for myself. I spent many hours watching television and reading fashion magazines so I could keep my pulse on the current season's trends.

It was bad enough that I could not go out and was missing from the social scene at Southern but I was also missing from clubbing back home. I wanted to be ready when I could venture back out and partake in my campus life and my nightlife.

I spent a lot of time in stores like Joanne's Fabrics and AC Moore craft store. Not only did I like to sew, I also liked making customized doll clothes. I had one doll that I named *Ma' Punk*. She was a combination of Claire Huxtable and my sister, Sìmone. That's where the name *Punk* part comes from. That was always a term of endearment that I called her. Our family shows love in the darnedest ways. I refer to my nephews, Simone's sons as monsters.

I have older nephews, Jahmai & Aaron and a niece, Tiana, from my sister Shandra. Tiana is actually named after me. She spells it differently. I jokingly say her name is spelled correctly and mine is spelled phonetically with a bunch of useless accent marks. My mother was intoxicated by French names and accents. I say this with a note of sarcasm while rolling my eyes.

I love all my nephews and niece but I felt a strong kinship and connection with Jeremiah back then and still do. It occurred to me that we were both trying to learn the same sets of skills at the same time. For example, we were both learning how to get around.

He was learning how to walk while I was re-learning how to walk. Some days he was doing better than me!

Jeremiah also featured in another habit that developed around this time. I had odd sleeping patterns still. Often I would fall asleep quickly but then wake up between two and four in the morning and could not get back to sleep. I had the worst case of insomnia for months.

This was in part because the metal rods I had at various points in my body, but especially my pelvis, they seemed to be poking me in my back. I just couldn't get comfortable. That's when I would struggle to the kitchen and make myself Pillsbury chocolate chip cookies. For some reason, Jeremiah would be awake too. He would sit in his highchair and join me in my pre-dawn snack while watching Good Times of all shows.

I was still on some medication, including Zoloft to help me with my sleep and mood. It didn't seem to be helping with either. I was still frustrated by my limitations. A nurse was coming to check my vitals and take blood daily, which meant that my severely abused veins continued to be a problem.

I am one to frequent the dentist often. I have sensitive teeth. But during this period, I couldn't have any dental work done. I couldn't even do the typical preventative regimen like getting my teeth cleaned and sealant applied.

I was on Coumadin, a blood thinner. Even getting my teeth cleaned was an issue. Could you imagine bleeding to death because of a dental cleaning? After all I had been through, "Death by Floss" was not going to be how I go out.

The winter days passed. Amy, my physical therapist, who had been so helpful while at the convalescent home, continued to get me moving. I was able to schedule my physical therapy at the facility where she worked full-time.

It was still a struggle but I was walking a little easier, using a cane and now afforded the dignity of being able to take care of my personal hygiene and dress without needing constant supervision. However, I was now getting frustrated with being so housebound. My mother would drive me places and I would accompany her on errands just to get out of the house.

One day, I announced to my mother that I wanted to go and visit my car. As I have mentioned, the car was still impounded by the Connecticut State Police but no longer in plain sight at the Troop G facility. It was at a garage now. They still hadn't destroyed it because it had been in an accident where there had been a fatality and thus had yet to be transported to the scrap yard.

Part of my motivation to see the wreckage came from wanting to salvage what I could from the car. Upon leaving the hospital, I had been given the remains of my clothes I was wearing on the night of the crash. They were mostly cut up and tattered as they had been removed once I got to the hospital and was being prepared for surgery. I still have those clothes to this day. I was still missing one of my shoes, however -- my Fendi sandal.

Seeing my car was a surreal experience. It was smashed even beyond what I had imagined.
I honestly couldn't fathom anyone surviving that crash and the fact that I had was, well, difficult to comprehend. I don't know if they cleaned it or if there ever was but I didn't see any blood.

I used to keep my car spotless but here it was a mangled, crushed disaster. It was cut in pieces because the Jaws of Life were used to cut me out of the wreckage. I searched inside what was left of my car but never did find my other shoe. However, I did salvage a CD that apparently I had been listening to that day. It was a CD by the rapper known as DMX, "It's Dark and Hell is Hot." For those who believe in synchronicity, you might like to know that 14 years later I met Earl Simmons, aka DMX, in person.

I was staying in the same hotel as he and so when I had a chance I introduced myself and told him about my accident. He then told me about an accident he had but he was the one driving under the influence of a substance let's say. Shortly after leaving his movie set, he crashed and totaled his brand new Mercedes. The only thing he was able to recover from it was...his own CD. We exchanged numbers and promised to keep in touch.

But traveling, meeting celebrities and staying in hotels was still a long way off for me in February 2000. I still didn't feel like the real me. I had to rediscover myself all over again and it seemed to be taking a very long time. I wanted my life back. Occasionally, some friends would offer to take me out and we would go to lunch or dinner. Of course, my mom was always there to remind them that I was still very fragile. And as much as I hated to admit it, I was. The girls would chauffeur me around with my cane as would my mom. I was getting fed up with it.

One afternoon, my mother took me to CVS so I could stock up on my medical supplies. As we were heading back to the car, I told my mother that I was going to drive her home. I don't think she was that surprised. She knew how frustrated I had become being so dependent on others. And remember, this was the mother, who tested me by asking me driving directions to our home when I was just four years old.

I thought that I would be fine driving but there was a nagging doubt. After all, that annoying psychiatrist had suggested that I might never be able to drive again or insinuated that if I did, it would take me a long time to get back behind the wheel. To add insult to injury, he said that if I eventually did so, I would be a neurotic mess. Would I? I may be paraphrasing a bit but that is my interpretation of what I heard him say.

I struggled into the driver's seat and strapped on my belt. I flipped on the ignition and then...I drove home. I didn't have one palpitation. I wasn't sweaty or anxious. If anything, I was relieved.

But that one big step forward made me even more determined to regain my former life. I missed my job and my friends. The campus was my life and I had been away from it for too long. I was getting particularly nostalgic because the basketball season was in full swing and I missed the games. I love basketball. Remember, I was a cheerleader in high school and worked in the Athletic Department at Southern. I organized the basketball pep rallies for Midnight Madness. So, after my successful return to driving I had an idea.

A few days after my trip back from the CVS pharmacy, I called Enterprise Rental Car Company and asked them to come and pick me up as I wanted to rent a car.

Following the write-off of my own car, I had thirty days rental car coverage on my auto policy and I decided I was now ready to take advantage of that provision.

When my mother saw the rental car, she almost flipped out. But I assured her I would be fine. I didn't tell anyone, except Sadia, I was coming as I headed off to campus. I had a lot of people to see and a basketball game to watch.

When I arrived on campus my friends were shocked to see me. I managed to navigate around with my cane and it was a relief to be back home surrounded by all the things that had become so familiar to me. I had been at Southern for almost eight years both as a student and now as an employee.
I felt very comfortable there. It was literally my home away from home.

The visit lifted my spirits but I still had a long way to go. I got tired very easily. Using a cane was demanding. I was still on meds. Sure, I was improving but not as fast I would have liked. One day, I took a good look in the mirror. I almost didn't recognize myself. I had lost a lot of weight. My usually round cheeks looked thin and gaunt. If you didn't know me all you saw was my great bone structure. After taking my weave out I saw that my hair was really thin and looked so unlike me that I made a decision to cut it all off!

My mood could also fluctuate. On one occasion, I slept through the arrival of visitors. My mother had cooked some barbeque chicken for dinner and by the time I woke up, my cousins and Aunt Adaire had eaten the chicken pieces that I liked. I freaked out. My mother suggested that I take another Zoloft but I was not amused. And it bothered me that any reactions of mine were now being interpreted as a result of the accident rather than naturally occurring emotions. It is not strange to have a preferred chicken part.

During the spring I continued my recovery and drove myself around when I had the energy. Yes, I even drove in the very spot, the entrance to the Merritt Parkway, where I had nearly been killed. It didn't make me anxious. If anything it made me wonder. I wondered why I was alive. I wondered why I had been saved.

My doctors called me their miracle patient. Many had never seen anyone recover from the type of injuries I sustained so I knew I had a purpose…but what? What was my purpose? Those questions took up residence in my consciousness and they appeared when my mind was not otherwise occupied. They still do…

The questions about my purpose spurred me to make even greater effort to move on with life and, more specifically, get back to work. I was determined to return as soon as possible.

I even eschewed disability because I was determined to make my life purposeful and not be restricted or defined by my accident.

My progress was slow but sure and occasionally punctuated by setbacks. In June I had to have hernia surgery. My doctors warned me I would need this surgery down the line and maybe more than once. Due to my abdominal wall being open I had a mesh screen inserted. A hernia can occur and cause a protrusion. When this happens they must operate.

For my first hernia repair, it couldn't be done laparoscopically back then, which meant it was more painful than it needed to be. I couldn't laugh for days without hurting and everyone was making me laugh for one reason or another. My buddy, Bucky, called to check on me when in the hospital and as usual, he made me laugh. Buck was always telling some humorous story.

My friends and acquaintances always made me feel like I lived a real Seinfeld episode. They're all a bunch of amusing characters.

By the time I recovered from the surgery I decided I was ready to go back to work. The relative inactivity, being constantly at home and the nagging questions about the meaning of my life, all conspired to push me back to work. And as I had now graduated and finished my master's degree, I was ready for the next phase.

I had indeed been able to participate with my class colleagues in the graduate school commencement ceremony in May. It was questionable whether I would be able to walk across the stage to receive my diploma. I knew I would be walking. I never doubted it. I walked across the stage and was handed my Master of Education Diploma from Dr. Sandra Holly, Dean of Graduate Studies.

Now, I was eager to resume my career.

I started back in July and my co-workers were happy to see me. They were also shocked. The reaction of Mark, the Director of Housing, was priceless. He looked like he was seeing a ghost when I walked in!

"Are you sure you have the doctor's clearance?" he asked in astonishment.

He told me about a dream he had after receiving the news about my car accident. He said I walked into the office, same as I did this morning but was badly bruised as they described to him after seeing me in the hospital. This dream coupled with his not being apprised of my return to work added to his shock. I assured Mark I was fine, though there were some of my previous duties I couldn't yet manage, like lifting anything, or being on call for emergencies. Because my activity was limited, I found myself doing more and more administrative work and less and less of the hands-on work that I loved.

At Southern, I had always felt that I was at the center of the action but now I felt on the periphery, moved to the side. That still doesn't work for me. I like being a part of the action even in my current position. I'm a hands-on type of person not a spectator. If I had a word for it, I'd say I'm a fixer – very results orientated. If you want resolution, call me, if you want to vent, call someone else.

Even though, my staff was just accommodating me and concerned for my better welfare, I didn't like not being able to participate in everything like before. To make matters worse, I was struggling with my mobility and my energy. My colleagues started to get concerned about me.

I had a decision to make. I was excited to be back on campus, in my apartment with my friends but I wasn't 100%. It was bad enough, I no longer had my huge director apartment at Wilkinson. I was now in a smaller apartment at Farnham. It was more of a Graduate Intern size apartment. The staff had taken care of my items but someone stole my twisted Corona beer bottle. I've never been to Mexico but many of the students traveled there for Spring Break. Someone brought back a cool, twisted neck bottle of Corona.

I had it on the shelf in my office and someone helped themselves to it while I was out. Amazing how people will just help themselves to your things when they think you may never return. Maybe they think they'll have a piece of you...No, that's not it.

You can probably tell by my tone I still get upset about it. My bottle was never returned and I never made it to Mexico to get another.

By the time school was back in session and full student life resumed on campus at the end of the summer, I was feeling overwhelmed and a bit disenchanted. After talking with my colleagues I decided I needed to take some time off. I had come back too soon. My bosses and I agreed that I should take the semester off and aim to return in January. This was one of the hardest decisions I ever made. I was so happy to be back and resume my life but the reality is I hadn't and maybe never would.

As I went back home from my job and on-campus apartment, I started to seriously consider the next steps for me. I had assumed I would find fulfillment with the resumption of my career at Southern. But perhaps that wasn't meant to be. Perhaps it was time to consider a new direction?

During the fall I thought long and hard about these issues. A friend suggested that we should both take the LSAT. Numerous people had told me that I should consider a career in law and now, with some free time to study, I gave the LSAT a shot. Lucy, a friend from SCSU and I took the LSATs at Fairfield University.

Our strategy was to take it with minor preparation then take a second time and consider Kaplan. In the interim, I applied for a job locally at the local community college. They had just done a major move to a new building downtown. I like having options.

I decided not to take the LSATs a second time. If I was going to apply, I was content with my score and didn't think Kaplan would increase it that much. Lucy on the other hand was determined and registered for Kaplan. I wasn't certain if I was going to actually go to law school but my strong sense, however, was that change was in the air. I just didn't know what form it would take. However, I like to keep busy, so while I cogitated on what my next step would be I didn't sit idle. After all those months in a hospital bed, I would likely never sit idle again.

I always liked to perform but the practical side of me prefers a steady paycheck, unfortunately, show business doesn't guarantee that. But, I always want to feed that creative side. Through a chance meeting with Juan, the Program Director at WYBC Radio, I realized I had a talent which grew into a love for being an on-air radio personality. I love music and performing so why not dovetail the two? I ended up being a DJ at WYBC for over four years.

EIGHT

Moving On

Hold fast to dreams for if dreams die, life is a broken-winged bird that cannot fly.
- Langston Hughes

In the fall of 2000 I was struggling. My premature return to Southern had proved to me that life wasn't yet the same as before my accident. Physically and emotionally, I was not the same person as I had been before September 1999. My natural inclination was to get back to that former state, to regain my former life. I loved my role on the campus, being with students, in an atmosphere of learning and activism. That was part of my identity and I felt very comfortable there.

Yearning to go back to how I was before my accident, including going back to my life at Southern, was born of a natural desire to move beyond my accident and put my flirtation with death firmly in the review mirror. However, I learned during that fall of 2000, that most times, to move forward in your life, you cannot go back. There's a reason the windshield is bigger than the rearview mirror. Where you're going is so much better than where you've been.

As much as I loved my life at Southern, I was beginning to wonder whether that chapter of my life was over. I was, however, having a hard time letting go. When I talked to my colleagues and friends, several of them suggested that perhaps life at Southern was too comfortable and maybe it was time to move on and look for new challenges. I agreed that being too comfortable at my age is not good. I needed new experiences.

When it was time to get a new car, I decided I wanted the exact same car that I had, even though it had been crushed in my accident. However, I had a friend whose father worked at the local Mercedes dealer, so I duly paid him a visit. While there, he explained that Mercedes had patented the "crumple-zone" in their cars, which meant that in the event of an accident, the engine dropped down to the ground, as opposed to smashing into the driver's cabin of the car and in my case crushing my lap. That sounded great but the problem was that I wanted my car fully loaded, and that effectively priced me out of a Mercedes.

I then paid a visit to Acura where my boss at Southern's brother-in-law worked in Sales. I really wanted another Acura. He told me that Acura no longer made the model that I had been driving but they had a new, sportier, six-cylinder version and it had -- a crumple zone. I was sold and soon back on the road in my new car, driving it without fear or anxiety.

Somewhat reluctantly, I applied for other jobs. I was offered a job as a store manager of a retail store in Manhattan. Didn't apply to that but they found me on Monster.com. I've always had an affinity for Manhattan but I didn't see myself commuting for retail, at least not that particular chain. Thinking back now, I could've parlayed it into a position at one of my preferred fashion houses but I don't think it was for me. Retail can be physically demanding and I needed a position that would not have such demands.

American Express also tried to hire me to be a Financial Advisor. Not sure what they saw in my resume to think I would be a good fit for that position. There were a few other offers but nothing that interested me. Then I was offered the job at the local community college in my home town. It is a two-year public community college and is one of twelve such schools, governed by the Connecticut Board of Regents. I was offered the job of Director of Student Life. Although, I had never stepped foot inside the school prior to interviewing for this position, I knew I could transition into it rather easily plus it was a state school so I would be able to continue to accrue time as a state employee.

The job offered more money than I was currently making but I was still apprehensive. I couldn't be sure whether my concerns were simply due to my comfort level and natural uncertainty about change or whether there was something more significant that I couldn't quite identify.

Most of my friends and colleagues were excited for me, however, and told me to go for it.

I accepted the position.

Saying goodbye to my friends, colleagues and my life at Southern was hard. I had spent almost a decade -- very formative years -- learning about education and myself. Even though, I was sad to go, saying goodbye was not difficult. I can't explain it but maybe because of my car accident, I don't have a hard time with goodbyes and I knew it was time to move to my next station in life. Southern and the people there, had been an integral part of my accident and recovery. The campus was my destination when I was hit head-on. My colleagues had sat vigil by my bedside during the entire ordeal. They had given me amazing love and support. They were my family. So leaving the job was not hard because I didn't think I would no longer be seeing them. Further, my accident taught me that life is short and things could change in a heartbeat. It was time to move on.

I prepared myself for my new journey. It certainly felt different heading to a new campus. I was confident in my abilities and in my experience but still unsure. I really didn't know anyone there which I thought was a good thing. It was time for a new chapter with new relationships.

The first two weeks were terrible! At Southern, people knew and accepted me for who I was but at the community college nobody knew me and my working style. They expected me to be like my predecessor. They thought I was just another employee, a new recruit who was expected to fit in.

At Southern, my energy and drive were known entities and, by and large, people appreciated them and let me run with them. I had freedom and was given latitude because I was trusted and results oriented. Sure, there were times when I could be headstrong, but my colleagues knew this. Here, I was expected to follow the rules, keep my head down, and just do my job. Moreover, as a two-year program, it wasn't as diverse or as active as Southern and its four-year and graduate programs but I understood this because it was not a university. Nonetheless, I was thoroughly miserable.

One day, during the first terrible couple of weeks at my new job, I consoled myself by going for lunch with one of my new friendly colleagues at a well-known Italian restaurant Downtown Bridgeport. The restaurant was often frequented by people from Southern and by pure chance, on this day, the President of Southern and his inner circle just happened to be there.

President Adanti, a man I respected, asked me "Hey Kid, how's the new job going?" Holding back tears because I felt such relief seeing him all the way in Bridgeport in the middle of my day, I responded, "It's not going well at all. I want to come back home?" I pleaded with all sincerity.

"No, because you have to give it some time," the President said wisely. "But, of course, you can always come back home," he added with a smile.

His response made me feel a lot better. I knew he was right. I did need more time. But I was comforted to know that I would always be welcomed back at Southern. The conversation restored my confidence and resolve. That day I decided I'm going to take on this new challenge head on and soon they'll think the Student Activities at this community college is equal to that of a university.

Needless to say, my acclimation to the college took some time. I started working there in July just a week after my Aunt Adaire passed away. Adaire is one of my mother's younger sisters and is my Uncle Adrian's twin sister. She is also my cousins, Deja, Dana, Deneisha and Dominique's mother. That loss was hard for our family. Her passing was unexpected.

In August I was asked if I would like to teach a course the upcoming fall at the community college. There was a need for additional instructors to teach a Developmental Studies course to first year students. My supervisor and Human Resources Director knew I had a Master of Education degree and previously taught so they thought I would be a great fit.

When most of the faculty returned at the end of the summer, some of the senior members were upset that I was teaching. At Southern, it was not that uncommon for someone in my position and my age to also teach but this was not the way it was done here. They thought I was too young among other things and maybe too *urban* let's say to have a master's degree. Well, they were wrong.

The structure seemed more rigid and no one seemed prepared to give this new recruit a chance. I might have been new to the staff and faculty at this local community college but I felt as if I had expertise and experience that was relevant and useful. Further, I had the same number of degrees in my twenties as the seasoned faculty did and there was nothing anyone could do to change that.

Some of the people at my new workplace didn't see it that way. Some of the faculty actually questioned whether I really had a master's degree. My mother being protective wanted to come to my office and post my degrees on the wall.

I told her I likely would have before my degree was questioned but now I refused to play into this. Education is the one thing no one can take from you and I earned mine. I don't need to prove it to anyone.

The mismatch between my skill and my superiors' expectations became clear when I was asked to create a new travel policy. I did my due diligence and created new guidelines for student travel abroad. I also knew that the policy would need to be approved by the State Comptroller's Office. I knew people in that office and promptly sent them a version of my newly constructed policy but first I called and asked what was mandatory to include.

The next day I got hell for not sharing my policy with my superiors and simply calling the State Comptroller's Office! Honestly, I wasn't being disrespectful. On the contrary, I thought I was being efficient. Once again, an attempt to make me feel inferior but it didn't work. My travel policy was adopted and I took the students on many trips including Montreal, Italy, England, Morocco and Spain.

I don't believe in impossible. If something is possible, I will get it done. If it is impossible you must explain to me why and it cannot be simply because it has never been done.
It always seems impossible until it is done.
– Nelson Mandela

If I was frustrated and feeling that I was being treated less than I deserved at work, the situation was completely reversed in another area of my life.

Ever since my accident, and particularly since my recovery, some people were seeing me in a different light. They interpreted the fact that I survived a horrific, head-on crash as a sign that I was special in some way. This was especially true in church. When I first hobbled back into church, people were not just happy to see me, they wanted to touch me. It was as if I had a special quality that everyone wanted to get a piece of.

I recall a family gathering in which my Aunt Thelma asked me very specifically to pray for her. "Of course", I said. However, when she asked me to lay my hands on her, I remember thinking to myself, I am not a prophet. She said, "I know you have a direct line to God," she said, reflecting a sentiment that a number of people shared.

Sometimes, I would get so much attention by just walking into church! I am not one for being the center of attention. I didn't like the implication that I was somehow special, although I was moved that my story seemed to be helping others in their faith. But I was uncomfortable. Moreover, this attention only made me obsess more about why I had been saved and what was my purpose? A combination of survivor's guilt and extreme gratitude made me question everything.

These feelings came to the forefront in 2001 when a male cousin, six years younger than I, committed suicide. Surely I should have seen the danger and saved him. This was my thinking despite the fact that rationally I knew I hadn't recently been in contact with him and I didn't know what he was going through at the time. I took it hard because it was a suicide of my younger cousin who I grew up with and only remember him laughing and smiling. I also believe my feelings were indicative of how focused I was on my life's meaning and purpose.

At the community college I needed to build my credibility and have people understand I am passionate about making a difference and doing a great job. Fortunately, my immediate supervisor, Edwena, thirty years older to the day -- we had the exact same birthdays -- did come to appreciate and understand me. She really appreciated my can-do attitude. My mantra, and to some extent my reputation, was based around a simple idea: *Don't tell me it can't be done*. I was creative in my solutions to problems and most of all, I had great follow-through. I wouldn't back down. I had confidence I could always find great solutions. I tackled my tasks head-on.

Gradually, the faculty and staff came to really appreciate my efforts and my approach at least that's what I told myself. I met some great people while there. Some I'm still good friends with to this day. One I miss dearly. My good friend Tony Ball who has since passed on but I truly miss him.

He was a genius or very close and everyone knew it. He had degrees from Princeton, Yale and Harvard and he thought I was bright. In fact, he asked me to co-teach a sociology course with him. Most of the faculty had a lot of respect and admired Tony. When they saw how much he admired and respected me, they took notice.

I knew some would never warm up to me and I was fine with that because I knew I was making an impact on student's lives. That is what mattered to me. Further, I was improving the quality of programming at the college as well. I brought such notable personalities as Maulana Karenga, the creator of Kwanzaa, Poet Laureate Amiri Baraka, poet and actor, Saul Williams and comedian, Kevin Hart.

I believe I was sent there to show these students the world is small but there are many experiences outside of this microcosm. To prove it, I took students on a day trip to Maryland. We left at 8:00 a.m. and took a comfortable coach to Maryland to the Blacks in Wax Museum, had a nice meal then headed back to Connecticut. We made it back before midnight. I wanted to show them they could travel four states away in less than a day! Some of these students had never been outside of Greater Bridgeport. So by the time I took them to Europe they were budding jet-setters.

As the Coordinator of Student Life, I realized I did more than this position entails so I worked to get a promotion and expand the title. Before I left I was the Director of Student Life & Activities and Special Admissions Projects. I've never been one to stay in my lane. If I see an area where I can lend my talents, I do.

I started working with the Dean of Outreach on marketing and recruiting projects for the college. I had innovative ideas on how to recruit students and entice them to register at the school.
One of my ideas caused the largest increase in students registering at this school ever!

That same Dean who admonished me for calling the Comptroller's Office when I first started commended me for a job well done and publically gave me all the credit. Well, he said I did a great job unless this whole thing was some sort of anomaly that he hasn't quite figured out. I'll take that and you're welcome.

Eventually, I found myself on the Steering Committee that was overseeing a huge development for the college -- a new addition to the school.
I realized I liked development. I took the real estate course at the school and acquired my real estate license and became a Realtor. I needed something to go to school for and I could take the course at no cost as an employee as long as it wasn't full.

Did I mention I acquired my Sixth Year Professional Degree in Educational Foundations while working at the community college already by this time? I found a way to spend time back on Southern's campus after all.

I took courses in the evening to acquire my Sixth-year Professional Degree. During my last project, my professor told me I was too creative to teach. Can you imagine that? I knew what he meant though. He said I should be in New York City doing something amazing and creative like in the fashion industry.

In his defense, instead of doing a boring Power Point like my classmates, I prerecorded my presentation with a hip jazz background and timed it so I didn't need to say anything. I stood at the podium pointing like Vanna White or a Price is Right model. But, I did take his advice. That summer I married my two loves and took a shoe design course in Manhattan at Parsons School of Design.

The whole expansion project at the college took four years. I was heavily involved in the new design, which featured the incorporation of a lot of smart technology and high tech gadgetry in and out of the classrooms. We were very proud of our media-rich classrooms. It was great seeing the evolution of the concept from design to fruition.

When the building was finally complete, I felt I had participated significantly in a major enhancement and advance for the college.

The President chose to stay in the old building and so I ended up in the best office suite with a spectacular view, in the new wing. I felt that I had accomplished a lot in my various roles at the college. However, I was also feeling that it was now time to move on. I believed that I had done all I could in my role and that it was time for new adventures.

Once again, I was left pondering my next career move.

NINE

New Beginnings

To live is the rarest thing in the world.
Most people exist, that is all
- Oscar Wilde

There was a special energy in the air this fall. The Presidential election has always been an exciting time for me. I have always been interested in politics. When I was in high school I said I'd run for President one day. Back then I didn't think I'd be the first Black or Woman President. I just thought I would be the next…

My students came to me with the idea of going to the president's inauguration in D.C.. Of course, this was before they knew who would win but many felt this inauguration would be extra special and surpass any other. Oddly, I initially had no desire to travel to D.C. and deal with the large crowds and cold weather but I liked their optimism and energy so I said I would look into it.

I was teaching an evening developmental course this semester and had a diverse mix of students not just ethnically but varying ages, socioeconomic status and academic ability. I had a safe zone culture in my class so all my students felt comfortable speaking freely but respectfully about all topics.

I encouraged them to keep abreast of current affairs local, national and international.

One day, a student wanted to talk about the presidential election. I welcomed this discussion but I first wanted to know who knew the candidates running? When I saw a divide between who was in the know and who was clueless, I realized this was a great learning opportunity and I would make it a teaching moment.

We discussed the candidates running both local and state level. We didn't focus on party affiliation but more on the candidates and the issues. I could see the lights going on behind their eyes and their genuine interest. I had students that admitted to never registering to vote and having no desire to change their minds a few weeks before the election. These same students decided to register just days before the election at the Registrar of Voters office because they now found their voice and wanted to use it.

My students had no idea I was moonlighting by working nights and weekends on a state election. I was proud to be working on a candidate's campaign that would be on the same ticket as Barack Obama. Regardless of what party you are affiliated with, the idea of the first African American President being elected made the 2008 campaign special--For some of us, magical.

As the election neared, I was grateful to my students for asking me to look into attending the inauguration. I reserved tickets on an Amtrak that would be leaving Bridgeport at 10:30 p.m..

We would arrive to Union Station in D.C. at 4:00 a.m.. We would hang out there then walk to the National Mall after a few hours. After the Inauguration we would depart from D.C. at 4:00 p.m. and be home by 9:30 p.m.. We would travel together and witness that historic moment in less than 24hrs.

What I was not prepared for was the turn of events that would take place between November 4th and January 2nd. After Barak Obama was elected as the 44th and First African American President of the United States, the Presidential Inauguration became a hot ticket! There was also this new attention being given to the newly elected officials in local, state and federal offices, specifically, the newly elected congressman that beat the incumbent that had been in office for over twenty years. This was a major upset for some and a welcomed change for others.

I received a call asking whether I would be applying for a position in the newly elected congressman's office. I had never considered it. My short answer was "No." A few days later I received a second call asking the same question with the added comment that I should really consider it.

By the third call I said, "I am a state employee with tenure. I can run down the college halls naked yelling fire and not get fired. Why would I take a job that is in jeopardy every two years?" This person said because you would be good at it, you're what's needed to represent the people of Bridgeport.

This reminded me of a comedy special I saw many years ago with Steven Wright. He said when he was young, he was watching TV and a Smokey the Bear commercial came on and Smokey pointed his finger saying, "Only You Can Prevent Forest Fires." He said he thought Smokey was talking directly to him and now he had a responsibility. So he started filling buckets of water and throwing them out his bedroom window. I too suddenly felt this huge responsibility to my community and that it was incumbent upon me to save the people of Bridgeport.

I submitted my resume because I am a firm believer in taking the interview. You always take the interview. You never know when and where an opportunity is going to present itself. Plus, I had a talk with God and knew after we completed the new building, my job here was done. I knew I had hit my pinnacle at the college but was not certain what my next challenge would be. Further, I was taking a group of students to Italy during the winter recess so I had that to focus on as well as the inauguration trip.

I met with the transition team leaders who were doing the hiring for the congressman's new staff. We met at a cozy coffee shop in SoNo. I thought they were great. We had a lovely conversation -- I had the spiced chai, but I left thinking I don't know if this is going to be it…my next station I mean. But the interview went fantastic! It didn't feel like an interview at all.

When you are gainfully employed there's a certain level of confidence you exude and you are interviewing them as well. After all, I was very comfortable in my current position so when and if I decided to leave, it would have to be for the right reasons.

The holidays were extra festive this year because we witnessed history. The First African American President and The First African American First Lady were going to be moving into The White House. Being a history major and teacher, this was everything to me. I learned the most from my teachers who were there and lived in the moment in which they taught about. I was going to stand in a classroom and teach my students about this monumental time someday.

I get a phone call from one of the leaders of the transition team asking if I would be interested in a second interview with the new Chief of Staff. I'm saying to myself, "Always take the interview." I reply, "Yes, I would love to schedule a second interview."

The transition team leader asks "Can you interview next week?" I said, "I'm flying out to Italy January 2nd and will not return for eight days." They said they would like to meet before I depart. I said "Ok, my flight is Friday afternoon and the van is picking us up at 1:00 p.m., I can meet at 11:00 a.m. for an hour. "

Sìmone gave me a ride to the interview and after dropped me at the school so I could head to JFK to catch my flight to Italy. I again felt good about the interview and Sìmone said to me before I got out her car, "I think you got it! I feel it." I said, "If it's meant to be it will be--I'm off to Italy!"

We had a seven hour nonstop flight to Rome. I could not wait to check in, shower and rest. Seven hours without communication with the world...I thought I would be going through withdrawals but I wasn't. After getting comfortable in my room, I called to retrieve my voicemails. I must have listened to the message at least four times.

I was offered the job in the new congressional office! I wasn't certain I heard the message correctly so I called and asked my new director to say it to me. Even then, I repeated the salary I thought I heard twice and had her repeat it back to me.

So I won't be rich and now getting paid once a month instead of bi-weekly but I will be a part of history.

I am going to work in the Obama Administration! The first perk, inauguration tickets! But what about my students?

The atmosphere in Union Station was magical. Everyone was there for the same reason, to witness Barack Obama take the oath and become The First African American President of the United States.
I was elated to be sharing this experience with my nephews, Jeremiah and Justice, my parents, Sìmone and Deja. This was poetic. It would be the last trip I would be taking with my students but it was a new beginning for me.

A few days before, I had sent a campus-wide email to all faculty & staff informing them of my resignation and a hand delivered letter to the Director of Human Resources. I informed everyone, I was grateful for the time spent at the college and I wouldn't be far. I did not disclose that I would only be across the street.

We arrived at 4:00 a.m. but were not tired. It was bitter freezing temperatures for D.C. but we weren't cold. We were too excited! After hanging out in Union Station for a few hours we headed out. It was awesome! It was truly a *had to be there* moment. There was such optimism in the air. Millions watched on television but we were there...together.
I declined to use my inauguration ticket because I wanted to spend the day with my family.
I kept it for prosperity.

Shantè T. Hanks

TEN

Namastè

Your journey has molded you for the Greater Good.
It was exactly what it needed to be.
Don't think you've lost time.
It took each and every situation you have
encountered to bring you to The Now.
And Now is Right on time.
-Asha Tyson

DENKYEM

Symbol of adaptability

As time passed the accident receded somewhat in the rearview mirror of my life but it was always there, ready to loom large for a moment or an hour or a day. Nonetheless, the actual behavior of driving was never a problem.

I am driven. I was often told I have no patience.
I believe my lack of patience is why instead of being in the hospital for six months like my doctors thought, I was home in four. Instead of taking a year to walk, I walked in less than four months. I walked across the stage to get my masters diploma and contrary to what that psychiatrist thought, I drive.

There are days when I feel that because I survived the accident, I'm indestructible. My mother always says, "You don't know how you looked lying in that hospital bed. If you did you wouldn't do that!" This applies to almost anything I do that concerns her. Every once in a while I'll feel daring. I don't play chicken in the street but I will challenge myself. I try to be sensitive to the fact that my accident did not only change my life forever but my family and friends as well. They saw me lifeless, bruised and swollen. I didn't.

Sìmone, seemed to make it through the ordeal unscathed but I recently remembered one day she visited me at the convalescent home and she had an emotional breakdown. She was holding Jeremiah in his car seat and her arms and legs just went limp. She just started crying uncontrollably. I recall her saying "No one knows what I'm going through...I have a sick sister, a baby, school..." While I was going through my ordeal, Sìmone was raising an infant, going to college and working. I remember feeling really bad for her at that moment.

I mention these occurrences because I don't think people realize decisions that they make in an instant can have a life-long impact on themselves and others. Rodrigo was only twenty years old at the time of our accident. His mother brought him here from Brazil to further his education. She expected him to come home with a college degree not in a casket. She didn't expect to receive a telephone call that her son died in a tragic car accident. No mother wants to receive that call. In this case, it was preventable.

I also have moments when I get angry about the accident. I did nothing wrong! I wasn't drinking and driving. I was being responsible, as always and trying to make it back to campus. I replayed the events of the day once I realized the actual day it occurred and think could I have done anything differently? I wouldn't have because I did nothing wrong! Neither I nor my family deserved this. I will forever be scarred by this accident.

I am inclined to think about the things I can no longer do. Physical limitations have caused me to give up my dream of professional boxing. Ironically, I can no longer do a cartwheel either. After all my hard work, but I could for a short time and it served its purpose. I don't have full supination in my wrists and suffer from pain in my ankles, knees and pelvis. But I'm not complaining.

I was warned that I may have trouble at airports when going through metal detectors. When I first started traveling I carried a letter from my orthopedic surgeon explaining my issue and where the metal is located. I no longer carry the letter but used to get very frustrated when I would be stopped by TSA to be searched. I can tell you which airports have the more sensitive detectors. Now, I request the Advanced Imaging Technology, the new TSA body scanners so they can see the metal in my body on the screen. I look like Titanium Woman.

When I think about my breaks, metal and scars, I don't stay upset or angry for long because it could have been far worse. Instead of State Trooper Johnston telling my parents to get to the hospital because I had been in a car accident, she could have been informing them that I had died on the scene of a tragic car accident on the Merritt Parkway at 3:06 a.m..

I am alive! I am blessed!

SANKOFA

Symbol of importance of learning from the past

Kellie's Letter

Kellie gave me a card at the Carpè Diem party with a letter folded inside. On the outside of the letter she wrote "Please read in private. Love you!"

September 18, 2009

Dear Shantè Tiannia,

I am very pleased to be here with you today celebrating your life. It's been 10 years since the horrible accident that nearly took you away from us. I can remember it like it was yesterday. I'm not sure if I've ever told you how I felt about the accident, but here it goes. The night before the accident we were supposed to go out to a club that the radio station was going to be at. I can't remember the name of the club but it was in Norwalk. I do remember that you were hosting Val's bridal shower on this same night.

You called me to see if we were still going out because it was getting late and we weren't sure if it was even worth making the trip down to Norwalk. We went back and forth with making a decision and in the end we decided to just take a ride down there.

When we finally arrived at our destination, the line was outrageous! We knew that by the time we were able to get inside it would be time for the club to close so we decided not to go in. We sat around for a little while watching the crowd, then we moved on to our next destination. We went to Stamford to another club, which I also cannot remember the name of. In any event, we just sat outside and mingled for a little while before heading back home.

I remember that you dropped Shonda and me off then headed to your mom's house. You went to get your laundry and I believe you finished watching the Apollo before you left your mom's and headed home to New Haven. The next thing you know, hours later, I woke up to a phone call saying you were in a very bad car accident and it didn't look good. Needless to say, I lost it.

My main purpose for writing this is to let you know that for a very long time I kind of blamed myself for what happened. Not for the accident itself because I had no control over that, but because I felt that when we were trying to decide whether to go out that night, I should have said "no". I felt that if I would have said "let's stay home" the accident would have never happened because you would not have been out on the road at that time. I'm doing better with those thoughts now, but still to this day wish that I would have said "no".

You have no idea how grateful that I am to God for giving you a second chance at life. I am also grateful to God that I am able to be here with you celebrating your life. You are truly a blessing. Due to our different schedules and routines as we deal with everyday life, we don't get to spend as much time together as we used to. Regardless, I want you to know that I love you with all of my heart and you are truly an ANGEL.

Smooches,
Kellie Reneè

Shantè T. Hanks

Post Script

There is no greater agony
than bearing an untold story inside of you.
-Maya Angelou

In writing this book, I had to revisit feelings and emotions that had been pushed back, way down in the tunnels of my mind. This book has not just been an experience for me but for my friends and family as well. There were details and occurrences that I was not aware of by design or due to my being in a coma.

I visited Dr. Ivy, who is now the Senior Vice President for Medical Affairs and Chief Medical Officer at Bridgeport Hospital. It was surreal to be able to talk to him and thank him for saving my life that fateful night. I'm so grateful to have been able to have that moment with him. It was like seeing an old friend.

I also visited Dr. Langeland not too long ago in his office for a check-up. I wanted to ensure the titanium was fine and whether I should consider having him remove it. He assured me that unless I'm having problems, I will be living with this metal for the rest of my life. As a side, I tried to get him to agree that the titanium adds about twenty extra pounds on the scale to my overall bodyweight. He laughed and said "No."
I said, "How about ten?" He said "Maybe five to seven."
I said, "I'll take that!"

It was important for my story to be told from my perspective and my point of view but it was also equally important for it to be accurate. With that said, I needed to see the official police accident report.

I contacted the local State Trooper barracks - Troop G to see if they had a copy of the report. They no longer had a copy at their location but they informed me because there was a fatality, the State Police Records Office would have it in archives.

I drove to Middletown to the Connecticut State Police main building to retrieve a certified copy of the report. It came in the mail within two weeks. I read the report while sitting in my car.

Oddly, I do a lot of thinking in my car. I actually take comfort in sitting in my car, while parked in my driveway when I get home at the end of my day. I have been known to sit in my car for an hour or two to unwind and process the day while listening to music. Everyone has their thing, I guess this is mine.

As I'm reading the report, I realize it never dawned on me that this is not just *my* accident report, but this is *the* accident report. Meaning, there are details about his car, his physical state at the scene, and the police contacting his friends and family regarding his death. There are even details about the call to his mother in Brazil to inform her of the death of her son and his friends going the hospital to identify their friend's body.

I was more affected by reading about *his* accident than mine. Because of this, although I am including contents of the official accident report, I blackout names to be respectful of Rodrigo and his family.

THE ACCIDENT REPORT

Check off or fill in appropriate information   **PERSON LEVEL**

(TRAFFIC UNIT #1) NAME OF PERSON ~~Rodrigo~~ Rodrigo	(TRAFFIC UNIT #2) NAME OF PERSON Hanks, Shante
PERSON TYPE ☒ DRIVER ☐ PASSENGER ☐ PEDESTRIAN	PERSON TYPE ☒ DRIVER ☐ PASSENGER ☐ PEDESTRIAN
LICENSE ENDORSEMENTS REQUIRED FOR THIS VEHICLE (drivers only) ☐ YES ☒ NO/ IF YES, COMPLIED WITH ☐ YES ☐ NO	LICENSE ENDORSEMENTS REQUIRED FOR THIS VEHICLE (drivers only) ☐ YES ☒ NO/ IF YES, COMPLIED WITH ☐ YES ☐ NO
COMPLIANCE WITH LICENSE RESTRICTIONS (drivers only) ☐ NOT RESTRICTED ☐ RESTRICTIONS NOT COMPLIED WITH ☐ RESTRICTIONS COMPLIED WITH ☐ RESTRICTIONS COMPLIANCE UNKNOWN	COMPLIANCE WITH LICENSE RESTRICTIONS (drivers only) ☐ NOT RESTRICTED ☐ RESTRICTIONS NOT COMPLIED WITH ☒ RESTRICTIONS COMPLIED WITH ☐ RESTRICTIONS COMPLIANCE UNKNOWN
EJECTION PATH (if person was ejected)	EJECTION PATH (if person was ejected)
EXTRICATION ☐ NOT EXTRICATED ☒ EXTRICATED	EXTRICATION ☐ NOT EXTRICATED ☒ EXTRICATED
TAKEN TO HOSPITAL OR TREATMENT FACILITY ☒ YES ☐ NO	TAKEN TO HOSPITAL OR TREATMENT FACILITY ☒ YES ☐ NO
ALCOHOL INVOLVED ☒ YES ☐ NO	ALCOHOL INVOLVED ☐ YES ☐ NO (Unknown)
METHOD OF ALCOHOL DETERMINATION ☐ BLOOD, BREATH, URINE ☐ PASSIVE ALCOHOL SENSOR ☐ PRELIMINARY BREATH TEST ☒ OTHER (state type) ☐ BEHAVIORAL Autopsy ☐ OBSERVED	METHOD OF ALCOHOL DETERMINATION ☐ BLOOD, BREATH, URINE ☐ PASSIVE ALCOHOL SENSOR ☐ PRELIMINARY BREATH TEST ☐ OTHER (state type) ☐ BEHAVIORAL ☐ OBSERVED
ALCOHOL TEST RESULT (BAC if known) 0.21 %	ALCOHOL TEST RESULT (BAC if known)
OTHER DRUG INVOLVEMENT ☐ YES ☒ NO	OTHER DRUG INVOLVEMENT ☐ YES ☐ NO
METHOD OF OTHER DRUG DETERMINATION ☐ BLOOD, URINE ☐ OTHER (state type) ☐ BEHAVIORAL ☐ DRUG RECOGNITION TECHNICIAN	METHOD OF OTHER DRUG DETERMINATION ☐ BLOOD, URINE ☐ OTHER (state type) ☐ BEHAVIORAL ☐ DRUG RECOGNITION TECHNICIAN
DRUG TEST TYPE & DRUG TEST RESULTS (state type & results)	DRUG TEST TYPE & DRUG TEST RESULTS (state type & results)

ADDITIONAL COMMENTS

The medical records for Shante Hanks are unavailable at this time.

STATE OF CONNECTICUT
DEPARTMENT OF PUBLIC SAFETY
DIVISION OF STATE POLICE
DPS 302 C REV 7/85

CONTINUATION OF INVESTIGATION REPORT

CASE NUMBER	INCIDENT TYPE	PROSECUTOR'S REPORT				
G-99-■■■■■■	FATAL	☐ HAS BEEN MADE	☒ SUPPLEMENTARY	☐ TE-OFFS	☐ ASSIST	☒ CLOSING

DATE AND TIME ASSIGNED: On Sunday, 09-19-99 at 0306 hrs. I was assigned by Troop G Deskman, Trooper Joseph Staurovsky # 1054 and Dispatcher, Julie Wilcoxson, via radio to investigate a two car accident.

TIME OF ARRIVAL: 09-19-99 at 0309 hrs.

SUPERVISOR: SGT. James Lynch # 295 arrived 0317 hrs.

PERSONNEL AT THE SCENE:

State Police Personnel: Troop G
TFC. Linda Johnston # 980 dispatched at 0306 hrs.
Assignment: primary investigator

Trooper Gutierrez # 1404 arrived 0310 hrs.
Assignment: photographs

TFC. Walter Melfi # 1246 arrived 0317 hrs.
Assignment: Accident Reconstructionist

Stratford EMS:
Crew Chief   Bruce Connery
Driver: Rocky Vitale
Dispatched: 0307 hrs.
Arrival: 0322 hrs. (scene)
Departed: 0351 hrs. (scene)
Arrival   0357 hrs. (Bridgeport Hospital)
Transported: Operator #2/Shante Hanks

Nelson Ambulance:
Driver: Kate Sadlier
Paramedic: Kenneth Pitts
Dispatched: 0322 hrs.
Arrival: 0346 hrs. (scene)
Departed: 0351 hrs. (scene)
Arrival: 0357 hrs. (Bridgeport hospital)
Paramedic Pitts rode to Bridgeport Hospital
with Stratford EMS

NOV 0 8

STATUS OF CASE	1. ACTIVE 2. ADMINISTRATIVELY	3. EXPANDED 4. EXCEPTED	5. INACTIVE 6. NO CRIMINAL ASPECT	CODE 3	(No. OF CLOSED HOURS RED MUST BE USED WHEN CODE 2 OR 4 IS USED.)	MAN HOURS INC 1 15
SUPERVISOR'S SIGNATURE	_Sgt. J. Lynch_ 11/6/99	ID NO.	INVESTIGATING OFFICER SIGNATURE TFC _Linda P. Johnston_	ID NO. 980	DATE OF REPORT 10-30-99	

MASTER COPY

STATE OF CONNECTICUT
DEPARTMENT OF PUBLIC SAFETY
DIVISION OF STATE POLICE
DPS 202 C REV 7/95

CONTINUATION OF INVESTIGATION REPORT

CASE NUMBER	INCIDENT TYPE	PROSECUTOR'S REPORT				
G-99-▮▮▮▮	FATAL	☐ HAS BEEN SENT ☒ SUPPLEMENTARY ☐ RE-OPEN ☐ ASSIST ☒ CLOSING				

Stratford Fire Department:
Incident # 44-10

Units:

E-2:
Acting Chief: Lt. Brian Williams
Firefighters:
FF Michael Giaquinto
FF Anthony Herbon
FF Thomas Demarco
arrived 0316 hrs.

Rescue-1
FF John Dofficy
FF Russell Cameron
arrived 0316 hrs.

E-4:
Lt. Thomas Layman
FF Anthony Lopez
FF Ronald Christy
arrived 0318 hrs.

F-3
Deputy Chief:Robert Wilcoxson
arrived 0330 hrs.

All fire units and personnel left the scene
at 0607 hrs.

Troop G Desk Personnel:
Deskman: TFC Joseph Staurovsky # 1054
Dispatcher: Julie Wilcoxson

LOCATION OF VEHICLES:

Vehicle #1 (Eduardo) came to rest on Rt.15 in
the left lane of the eastbound lane, facing
in a northeasterly direction.

Vehicle #2 (Hanks) came to rest On Rt. 15
eastbound, with its front end partially in
the right and its rear end on the bridge
abutment of the Huntington Road Underpass.

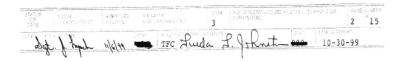

STATUS OF CASE	☐ ACTIVE ☐ UNFOUNDED ARREST ☐ SUSPENDED ☐ NOT CLEARED A. ROADTYPE B. OR DRIVING EFFECT	CODE	- AGE OF OLDEST INVOLVED MALE (IF AUTO WHEN CODE 2 OR 4 IS USED)	PAGE NUMBER	
		3		2	15
Sgt. J. ▮▮▮▮ 11/6/99 ▮▮▮	ID NO.	FULL OFFICER PRINTING SIGNATURE TFC Linda L. Johnet	ID NO.	DATE OF REPORT 10-30-99	

MASTER COPY

Shantè T. Hanks

CONTINUATION OF INVESTIGATION REPORT

CASE NUMBER: G-99-

INCIDENT TYPE: FATAL

PROSECUTOR'S REPORT: ☐ HAS BEEN SENT ☒ SUPPLEMENTARY ☐ RE-OPEN ☐ ASSIST ☒ CLOSING

LOCATION OF OPERATORS:
Operator #1 was found with his upper torso out the drivers window, his arms and head facing downward. His legs were twisted and trapped under the dashboard.

Operator #2 was trapped in the driver's seat with only her head and shoulders visible. Her vehicle was wrapped around her.

STATEMENT OF OPERATORS:
Operator #1 (████████) was deceased at the scene.

Operator #2 (Hanks) as of this writing does not remember details of the accident.

LOCATION OF PASSENGERS:
No passengers were present in either vehicle #1 or #2.

STATEMENT OF WITNESSES:
There were no reported witnesses to this accident.

POINT OF IMPACT: The exact point of impact could not be determined but based on the debris at the scene and the gouge marks located in the pavement it occurred near the white line separating the left lane from the right lane of travel. Refer to sketch map submitted by TFC. Melfi.

EXHIBITS:
1. Vehicle #1/Mitsubishi Eclipse, green, vin # ██████████████ Massachusetts marker # 5554KZ

2. Vehicle #2/ Acura 23CL, silver, 2 door sedan, Vin # ██████████████, Connecticut marker # 324 MYV.

3. One microcassette tape: 911 call of a wrong way driver on Rt. 15 E/B recorded on 09-19-99 at 0301 hrs.

STATUS OF CASE: 1. ACTIVE 2. CLEARED ARREST 3. SUSPENDED 3. A CLEARED 4. UNDER 5. NO CRIMINAL ASPECT

CODE 3

DATE OF REPORT: 10-30-99

PAGE NUMBER: 3 OF 15

TFC Linda L. Johnston

154

TITANIUM *Woman*

CONTINUATION OF INVESTIGATION REPORT

CASE NUMBER	ACCIDENT TYPE	PROSECUTOR'S REPORT				
9-99-	FATAL	☐ HAS BEEN SENT	☒ SUPPLEMENTARY	☐ PENDING	☐ ASSIST	☒ CLOSING

PHOTOGRAPHS: Photographs of this accident were taken by Trooper Gutierrez # 1404 of Troop G. Photo report is to be submitted by Trooper Gutierrez.

CONDITION OF OPERATORS: Operator # 1 was deceased at the scene.

Operator # 2 sustained multiple blunt trauma at the time of the accident and was transported via ambulance to Bridgeport Hospital where she was listed in critical condition.

CONDITION OF VEHICLES: Refer to inspection reports of Trooper Melfi for complete descriptions of damage sustained by Vehicles #1 and #2.

VEHICLES TOWED: Vehicle #1 was towed to Troop G by Jerry's Auto Body located at 1673 Stratford Ave, Bridgeport. CT., tel. # (203) 333-3361.

Vehicle #2 was towed to Troop G by Anthony's Auto Body located at 1750-1790 Stratford Ave. Bridgeport, CT., tel. # (203) 384-0001.

MEDICAL EXAMINER: ME Case # 99-10110
Medical Examiner: Anthony Giangrasso was notified by Troop G at 0400 hrs. he pronounced Operator #1, Rodrigo Eduardo, DOB: 12-22-78, dead upon his arrival at the scene at 0430 hrs. he cleared the scene at 0545 hrs. Office of Chief medical Examiner was notified by Dr. Giangrasso at 0600 hrs. requesting an autopsy.
A letter was sent on 09-19-99 requesting the complete autopsy results.

155

Shantè T. Hanks

CASE NUMBER	INCIDENT TYPE	PROSECUTOR'S REPORT				
G-99-█████	FATAL	☐ HAS BEEN SENT ☒ SUPPLEMENTARY	☐ RE-OPEN	☐ ASSIST	☒ CLOSING

UNDERTAKER: The body of the deceased, Rodrigo █████, was removed from the scene at 0526 hrs. and transported to St Vincent's Hospital by George J. Peterson funeral Home located at 1041 Noble Ave. Bridgeport, CT., tel. # (203) 384-8735.

TIME SCENE CLEARED: On 09-19-99 at approximately 0610 hrs.

NOTIFICATION OF NEXT OF KIN: On 09-19-99 at approximately 0630 hrs, Trooper Mohl # 1388 and Trooper Buinauskas # 1154 of Troop A went to the residence of Operator #1, Rodrigo █████, at 5 cross Street in Danbury in an attempt to make the death notification. They met with the victim's friend, Tavares █████, and encountered a language barrier. At 0645 hrs. the employer of the victim, Robson █████ arrived at Cross Street and was informed of the victim's death and he notified the victim's parents in Brazil. On Monday 09-20-99 at approximately 0620 hrs, Trooper Goncalves #1392 of Troop G was able to verify that his parents had been notified of their son's death, via telephone # █████ Trooper Goncalves spoke with Carlos █████ the step father of Rodrigo █████. Refer to the supplemental report of Trooper Goncalves for additional information.

IDENTIFICATION OF DECEASED: On 09-19-99 at approximately 0900 hrs. positive identification of the deceased Rodrigo █████ was made at St. Vincent's Hospital in Bridgeport by his friends, Flavia █████ of 9 South Well Street in Danbury and Robson █████, of 49 Chestnut Street in Danbury. The positive identification was made in the presence of St Vincent's Administrative Supervisor, Kathy Spillane. Due to the fact that I was not

TFC Linda L. Johnston 10-30-99

Page Number 5 of 15

MASTER COPY

156

TITANIUM *Woman*

STATE OF CONNECTICUT
DEPARTMENT OF PUBLIC SAFETY
DIVISION OF STATE POLICE
DPS-302-C REV. 7-96

CONTINUATION OF INVESTIGATION REPORT

CASE NUMBER	INCIDENT TYPE	PROSECUTOR'S REPORT				
G-99-	FATAL	☐ HAS BEEN SENT	☒ SUPPLEMENTARY	☐ RECEIVED	☐ ASSIST	☒ CLOSING

present at the time the identification was
made, TFC Orama # 1060 of Troop A in Southbury
went to the ▓▓▓▓ residence in Danbury on 09-
19-99 at approximately 1430 hrs. and took a
written statement from Flavia ▓▓▓▓ to verify
the positive identification. Refer to the
statement of Flavia ▓▓▓▓.

POSTMORTEM
EXAMINATION:

On 09-19-99 beginning at 1301 hrs. and ending
at 1401 hrs., a post mortem examination was
performed by H. Wayne Carver, II, M.D., Chief
Medical Examiner, on the body of Rodrigo
▓▓▓▓ at the Office of Chief Medical
Examiner, 11 Shuttle Road in Farmington.
The cause of death was listed as Multiple
Blunt Traumatic Injuries, the injuries
included:
1. Laceration of the brain stem.
2. Fracture of thoracic spine.
3. Multiple rib fractures.
4. Lacerations of the aorta.
5. Laceration of thoracic spinal cord.
6. Lacerations and contusions of the lung.
7. Laceration of the liver.
8. Laceration of the spleen.
9. Avulsion of the large bowel from
   retroperitoneal attachments.
10. Fracture of the pelvis.
11. Fracture of the left femur.

Lab # L99-▓▓▓▓
The following findings are based on the
laboratory specimens taken from the deceased
during the postmortem examination:
1. Based on blood analyzed from the right
   pleural cavity there was an ethanol
   concentration of 0.21 % by weight.

2. The brain was also analyzed for the
   presence of ethanol and the concentration
   of ethanol found was 0.18% by weight.

Finding: Acute Ethanol Intoxication.

TPC *Luela L. Johnston*   10-30-99

Shantè T. Hanks

CONTINUATION OF INVESTIGATION REPORT

CASE NUMBER	INCIDENT TYPE	PROSECUTOR'S REPORT				
G-99-	FATAL	☐ HAS BEEN SENT	☒ SUPPLEMENTARY	☐ RE-OPEN	☐ ASSIST	☒ CLOSING

Blood was also screened for the presence of carbon monoxide and cocaine/cocaine metabolites, none were detected.

The copy of this Postmortem Examination report was received by this Trooper on 10-13-99.

24 HOUR BACKGROUND: On 09-26-99 at approximately 0030 hrs. the following information was provided by Flavia ▓▓▓▓, to this Trooper who interviewed her and took a written statement.

Mrs. Flavia ▓▓▓ has been a friend of the deceased, Rodrigo ▓▓▓, since he arrived in Connecticut from Brazil (Brasil) in April 1997.

Mrs ▓▓▓ stated that on 09-17-99 Mr. ▓▓▓ slept at his home at 5 Cross Street in Danbury. On 09-18-99 he worked at his job at Green Life Landscaping in Wilton from 0800 hrs. until 1400 hrs. Mrs ▓▓▓ stated that at approximately 1600 hrs. he came to visit her at 49 Chestnut Street in Danbury stayed for about an hour and left at 1700 hrs. to go home. She further stated that at 1800 hrs. Mr. ▓▓▓ arrived at the Miracelly beauty Salon in Danbury for a haircut and left there at 0630 hrs. Mrs. ▓▓▓ stated that she believed that he went home and in fact this was verified by Solange ▓▓▓, who also lives at 5 Cross Street in Danbury. Mrs. ▓▓▓ also stated that Mr. ▓▓▓ left home at 2000-2030 hrs. to go to the Miss Brasil Contest at the Italian Community Center located at 4000 Park Street in Bridgeport. Mrs. ▓▓▓ stated that she did not see Mr. ▓▓▓ again at midnight on 09-19-99 at the Community Center and that the last time she saw him was at approximately 0145 hrs. when she and her husband left the Community Center. Mrs. ▓▓▓ stated that Rodrigo ▓▓▓ did

STATUS OF CASE	1 ACTIVE 2 CLEARED ARREST	3 SUSPENDED 4 CLOSED	5 FUGITIVE 6 NO CRIMINAL ASPECT	CODE 3	AGE OF OLDEST ACCUSED (MUST BE USED WHEN CODE 2 OR 4 IS USED)	PAGE NUMBER OF 7 15

SUPERVISOR ... 11/6/99 ... TFC Luda P. Johnston ... 10-30-99

MASTER COPY

158

STATE OF CONNECTICUT
DEPARTMENT OF PUBLIC SAFETY
DIVISION OF STATE POLICE
DPS-332-C REV. 7/95

CONTINUATION OF INVESTIGATION REPORT

CASE NUMBER	INCIDENT TYPE	PROSECUTOR'S REPORT				
G-99-	FATAL	☐ HAS BEEN SENT	☒ SUPPLEMENTARY	☐ RE-OPEN	☐ ARREST	☒ CLOSING

not know his way around Bridgeport very well and that he had gotten lost going and coming from the same Miss Brasil Contest on Park St. in 1998. A friend of Mr. ████████ named Benedetti told Mrs. ████████ that the reason Mr. ████████ did not arrive at the Miss Brasil Contest until midnight this time (09-19-99) was because he also got lost on the way to 4000 Park Street even though he had a map. Mrs. ████████ did not know the complete name of Benedetti as Mr. ████████ had always addressed him as Bene. The Miss Brasil Contest ended at 0200 hrs., from that time until the time of the accident at approximately 0306 hrs. none of his friends could account for his activities.

WEATHER
CONDITIONS:
On 09-19-99 at approximately 0306 hrs, it was clear and dry with temperatures in the forties. According to the Ct. Weather center there was 1/8 of a mile of fog in low lying areas.

Geographical
Conditions:
Rt. 15 eastbound at the Huntington Underpass is a limited access highway with two lanes of asphalt surfaced roadway. On the right is a narrow asphalt shoulder like area along the base of the bridge abutment, with wooden guard rails on each side of it. On the left is a grassy median divider with a wooden guard rail. The lanes and narrow shoulders are clearly marked with brightly painted lane markers. There is no illumination on this section of the highway.

ACTION TAKEN:
On 09-19-99 at approximately 0306 hrs. I was assigned by Troop G Dispatcher, Julie Wilcoxson to investigate the complaint of a wrong way driver on Rt. 15, initially stated as Exit 47 in Trumbull and described as a green Eagle Talon, with a foreign looking operator who was driving westbound in the

STATUS		SUPERSEDED		FINAL		DOB	HOW IT WAS DISTRIBUTED (AND EXCLUDED WHEN KNOWN		PAGE NUMBER
☐ ACTIVE	☐ CLEARED ARREST	S	☐ CLEARED	F	☐ UNFOUNDED	3	3		8 of 15

TFC ████ Linda L. ████ ████ 10-30-99

Shantè T. Hanks

CASE NUMBER	INCIDENT TYPE	PROSECUTOR'S REPORT				
G-99-	FATAL	☐ HAS BEEN SENT	☒ SUPPLEMENTARY	☐ RE-OPEN	☐ ASSIST	☒ CLOSING

eastbound lane. A second dispatch was issued
a short time later stating that a two car
accident involving a wrong way driver had
occurred on Rt.15 eastbound between Exits 52
and 53.

Upon my arrival at the scene at 0309 hrs. I
observed a 1995 green Mitsubishi Eclipse
bearing MA marker # ████, with heavy front
end damage, facing in a northeasterly
direction, in the left lane. Operator #1,
tentatively identified by his CT operator's
license (█████ as Rodrigo █████, was
found with his upper torso hanging face down
out the driver's window and his lower torso
twisted and trapped under the dashboard. I
examined this Operator for signs of life and
determined that he was deceased. Vehicle # 2,
a 1998 silver Acura 23 CL bearing Ct. marker #
████ with heavy front end damage was
positioned with its front end facing in a
northeasterly direction partially in the right
lane and its rear end on the bridge abutment
of the Huntington Road Underpass. Operator
#2, tentatively identified by her Ct.
Operator's license (█████ as Shante
Hanks, was trapped in the driver's seat with
her vehicle wrapped around her, only her head
and shoulders were visible, she was conscious
and able to verbalize her concerns.

Additional personnel began to arrive at the
scene in the order and times stated above.
Upon arrival of the Stratford Fire Department
at 0316 hrs. they immediately began to
extricate Operator #2 (Hanks). At 0351 hrs.
Operator #2 was transported to Bridgeport
Hospital and arrived at the hospital at 0357
hrs. where she was examined by Karin Van
Gelder MD and found to have sustained multiple
traumatic injuries.

The Stratford Fire Department then extricated
Operator #1 █████ from his vehicle. At

DATE OF REPORT 10-30-99

PAGE NUMBER 9 OF 15

160

STATE OF CONNECTICUT
DEPARTMENT OF PUBLIC SAFETY
DIVISION OF STATE POLICE
DPS-308-C REV. 7/99

CONTINUATION OF INVESTIGATION REPORT

CASE NUMBER	INCIDENT TYPE	PROSECUTOR'S REPORT				
G-99- ▓▓▓	FATAL	☐ HAS BEEN SENT	☒ SUPPLEMENTARY	☐ RE-OPEN	☐ ASSIST	☒ CLOSING

0430 hrs. Anthony Giangrasso M.E. arrived at
the scene and pronounced Rodrigo Eduardo dead.
At 0526 hrs. the deceased was removed from the
scene by Peterson's Funeral Home and
transported to St. Vincent's Hospital.

Upon his arrival at the scene, supervisor Sgt.
James Lynch, assigned Trooper Gutierrez to
take photographs, and TFC Walter Melfi,
Accident Reconstructionist, to construct a
detailed sketch map and the post collision
vehicle inspections. After a thorough
inspection of the accident scene this Trooper,
and Trooper Gutierrez assisted TFC Melfi with
measurements. Refer to the sketch map of TFC
Melfi for a detailed description of the scene.

Both vehicles were towed from the scene to
Troop G for post collision inspections.
Vehicle #1 ▓▓▓▓▓▓ was towed by Jerry's Auto
Body and Vehicle #2 (Hanks) was towed by
Anthony's Auto Body. Refer to the post
collision inspection reports of Vehicle #1 and
Vehicle #2 submitted by TFC Melfi.

At 0607 hrs. the scene was cleared and I went
to Bridgeport Hospital to check on the status
of Operator #2, (Hanks). The hospital
personnel related that she was in critical
condition having sustained multiple blunt
traumatic injuries, including a fractured
pelvis, long bone fractures and there was the
presence of blood in her abdomen and that she
was currently in surgery.

Despite an ongoing effort by this Trooper to
contact relatives of both Operators it was
difficult. At 0705 hrs. I went to the last
known address of Shante Hanks, ▓▓▓▓▓▓▓▓▓▓
▓▓▓▓▓▓▓▓▓▓ and at 0710 hrs. I arrived
at that address and spoke with her step
father, Barry Shepard, ▓▓▓-▓▓-▓▓-▓▓ and her
mother, Robin Shepard, notifying them of the
motor vehicle accident, their daughter's

STATUS OF CASE	☐ ACTIVE ☐ CLEARED ARREST	☐ UNFOUNDED ☐ INACTIVE	☐ POSITIVE ☐ NO CRIMINAL ASPECT	CODE 3	ARE CHARGED ADVISED MUST BE USED WHEN CODE 5 OR 6 IS USED	PAGE NUMBER 10 OF 15

STATE OF CONNECTICUT
DEPARTMENT OF PUBLIC SAFETY
DIVISION OF STATE POLICE
JPS-302-C REV. 7/96

CONTINUATION OF INVESTIGATION REPORT

CASE NUMBER	INCIDENT TYPE	PROSECUTOR'S REPORT				
G-99-■■■■■■	FATAL	☐ HAS BEEN SENT	☒ SUPPLEMENTARY	☐ RE-OPEN	☐ ASSIST	☒ CLOSING

condition and her admittance at Bridgeport
Hospital. I also spoke with her sister, Simone
Hanks, who verbally stated that on 09-18-99
Shante was at a bridal shower at the Savin
Rock Conference in West Haven from about 1900
hrs. until 2310 hrs. On 09-19-99 at
approximately midnight she arrived at 145
Clover Street in Bridgeport and except for a
brief trip to Norwalk at approximately 0120
hrs., where she and her friend Kelly Milton
attempted to go to a night club, but did not
go in due to it's crowded condition. She
returned to the home of her mother until
approximately 0300 hrs. when she left to go to
New Haven where she is employed as the
Director of Wilkinson Hall at Southern
Connecticut State University.

On 09-19-99 at approximately 0630 hrs.
Troopers Mohl and Buinauskas of Troop A in
Southbury, went to the last known address of
the deceased, Rodrigo ■■■■■■ to notify his
friends of his demise, at which time the
Troopers encountered a language barrier. The
friends contacted, Flavia ■■■■■ and Robson ■■■
■■■■ who translated the information. At
approximately 0900 hrs. Mrs. ■■■■■ and Mr.
■■■■■■ went to St. Vincent's Hospital to
make a positive identification of the
deceased, due to the fact that his parents
were residing in Brazil. Because the staff at
St. Vincent's Hospital did not advise this
Trooper of their arrival to make a positive
identification as requested, TFC Orama of
Troop A, was assigned to get a written
statement from Mrs. ■■■■■■ related to the
positive ID of Rodrigo ■■■■■■. Refer to the
written statement of TFC Orama and the
Positive Identification section of this
report.

On 09-20-1999 at 0620 hrs. Trooper Goncalves,
who is fluent in Portuguese, made contact with
the parents of the deceased, who currently

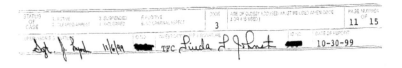

| STATUS OF CASE | 1. ACTIVE 2. CLEARED ARREST | 3. SUSPENDED 4. UNCLEARED | 5. POSITIVE 6. NO CRIMINAL ASPECT | CODE 2006 | AGE OF DECEASED (MUST BE USED WHEN CODE 2 OR 6 IS USED) 3 | | | PAGE NUMBER 11 OF 15 |
| SUPERVISOR'S SIGNATURE | | | ID NO. ■■■■ | INVESTIGATOR'S SIGNATURE TFC Linda L. Johnst ■■■■ | ID NO. | DATE OF REPORT 10-30-99 | |

Sgt. J. ■■■ 11/6/99

STATE OF CONNECTICUT
DEPARTMENT OF PUBLIC SAFETY
DIVISION OF STATE POLICE
DPS-DC REV 7/98

CONTINUATION OF INVESTIGATION REPORT

| CASE NUMBER G-99- | INCIDENT TYPE FATAL | PROSECUTOR'S REPORT ☐ HAS BEEN SENT | ☒ SUPPLEMENTARY | ☐ RE-OPEN | ☐ ASSIST | ☒ CLOSING |

reside in Brazil, to confirm that they were
notified of their son's demise as stated by
Mrs. Flavia ▇▇▇ He spoke with the step
father, Carlos ▇▇▇ who had
in fact been contacted prior to this date by
Robson ▇▇▇

On 09-19-99 a request for the Medical
Examiner's Report of Rodrigo ▇▇▇ was
forwarded to the Office of the Chief Medical
Examiner, case #▇▇▇ by this Trooper.
On 10-13-99 I received a copy of that report.
It listed the cause of death as multiple blunt
traumatic injuries. It attributed the manner
of death to the accident and described the
condition of Acute Ethanol Intoxication as
present. Refer to the post mortem section of
this report.

On 09-20-99 a dictalog tape of the 911 call
made to Troop G on 09-19-99 at 0301 hrs.
indicating the presence of a wrong way driver
on Rt. 15 at Exit 47 in Trumbull was taken out
of service. On 10-04-99 this Trooper made a
microcassette of that call and entered it as
evidence exhibit #3 on that date.

On 09-26-99 at 0030 hrs. I arrived in Danbury,
interviewed and took a written statement from
Flavia ▇▇▇ in which she related the 24 hour
period prior to the demise of Rodrigo ▇▇▇
It is significant that Mr. ▇▇▇ was not
familiar with the Bridgeport area and had
apparently gotten lost going to the Miss
Brasil Contest on Park Ave in Bridgeport for
two consecutive years. This time it is
believed by Flavia ▇▇▇ and other friends
that he was lost at some point from the time
he left Danbury on 09-18-99 until his arrival
at the contest in Bridgeport at 2355 hrs.
Refer to the written statement of Flavia
▇▇▇ and 24 hr. background section of this
report.

163

STATE OF CONNECTICUT
DEPARTMENT OF PUBLIC SAFETY
DIVISION OF STATE POLICE
DPS-302 C REV. 7/96

CONTINUATION OF INVESTIGATION REPORT

CASE NUMBER	INCIDENT TYPE	PROSECUTOR'S REPORT					
G-99-███████	FATAL	☐ HAS BEEN SENT	☒ SUPPLEMENTARY	☐ RE-OPEN	☐ ASSIST	☒ CLOSING

On numerous occasions I spoke with Bridgeport
Hospital personnel and Robin Shepard mother of
Shante Hanks in reference to Miss Hank's
medical status. After her initial surgery she
had chest tubes inserted and was placed on a
respirator. She had numerous surgeries in an
attempt to repair the extensive injuries
sustained during the accident. Miss Hanks had
been unable to verbally communicate for some
time due to the presence of the ventilator.

On 10-12-99 at approximately 1530 hrs. I
spoke via telephone to Robin Shepard and she
stated that Shante was off the respirator and
on a ventilator. I asked her if I could get a
signed consent for the medical records of
Shante Hanks and she stated that she would
contact her attorney and advise me. On 10-14-
99 I contacted Robin Shepard via telephone and
she stated that Shante and her attorney had
consented. At approximately 0730 hrs. I went
to Bridgeport Hospital and verbally
interviewed Shante Hanks, she stated that she
does not remember any of the accident or the
events leading up to the accident. Shante
signed the consent for her medical records but
although I was able to review her records to
date, I was unable to get a copy of them until
she is released from the hospital. As of this
date 10-27-99 she remains an in house patient
at Bridgeport Hospital, present status is
stable. Her medical records revealed that she
had fractures of the right wrist, right ankle,
fibula, left femur, multiple pelvic fractures
and a mesenteric laceration. A laboratory test
dated 09-19-99 taken at 0410 hrs. revealed a
blood alcohol of 0.01 gm/dl. a miniscule
amount. I will obtain a copy of her medical
records upon Miss Hanks release from
Bridgeport Hospital.

STATUS OF CASE	1. ACTIVE 2. CLEARED/ARREST	3. SUSPENDED 4. UNCLEARED	5. PUNITIVE 6. NO CRIMINAL ASPECT	CODE 3	AGE OF OLDEST ACCUSED (MUST BE USED WHEN CODE 1 OR 4-3 USED)	PAGE NUMBER OF 13 15

SUPERVISOR SIGNATURE Sgt. J. ██████ 11/6/99   ID NO. ████   INVESTIGATING OFFICER SIGNATURE TFC ██████ ████ ID NO. ████ DATE OF REPORT 10-30-99

TITANIUM *Woman*

STATE OF CONNECTICUT
DEPARTMENT OF PUBLIC SAFETY
DIVISION OF STATE POLICE
DPS-302-C REV 2/95

CONTINUATION OF INVESTIGATION REPORT

CASE NUMBER	INCIDENT TYPE	PROSECUTOR'S REPORT				
G-99-██████	FATAL	☐ HAS BEEN SENT ☒ SUPPLEMENTARY	☐ RE-OPEN	☐ ASSIST	☒ CLOSING	

CONTRIBUTING FACTORS:

Contributing factors in this fatal accident include:

1. A 911 tape, report of a wrong way driver near Exit 47, which was possibly Park Ave., the area from which operator #1 was coming from. The tape further provided a description of a similar vehicle, Eagle Talon, the same color (green) as the ██████ vehicle, with an Indian looking operator.

2. Although TFC Melfi was unable to establish the exact point of impact, gouge marks were located near the center of the two eastbound lanes, and is believed to be an indicator of the point of maximum engagement of the two vehicles. This indicates that Vehicle #1 (██████ and Vehicle #2 (Hanks) were involved in a head-on collision. This is supported by the fact that both vehicle #1 and #2 sustained heavy left front end damage with the most severe areas left of center with the vehicles twisted toward the left. With the heavily damaged area of both vehicles, left front, it is apparent that the vehicles were traveling in opposite directions. Vehicle #1 was traveling the wrong way, westbound in the eastbound lanes. Vehicle #2 had just entered the highway at entrance ramp #52 and was eastbound in the right lane of the eastbound lanes. Speed of either vehicle was not established.

3. Based on the Autopsy report of Dr. Wayne Carver M.D., Chief Medical Examiner, operator #1 ██████ was under the influence of an alcoholic beverage to the point of acute ethanol intoxication.

STATUS OF CASE	1. ACTIVE 2. CLOSED/ARREST	3. SUSPENDED 4. CLOSED 5. ADDITIONAL ARREST	CODE 3	THIS OR OLDEST ACTIVERS MUST BE USED WHEN CODE 2 = 4 OR CODE 5	PAGE NUMBER 14 15

Sgt. J. ███ 11/6/99 ██ TFC *Linda L. Johnston* ██ 10-30-99

165

Shantè T. Hanks

STATE OF CONNECTICUT
DEPARTMENT OF PUBLIC SAFETY
DIVISION OF STATE POLICE
DPS-302-C REV 7/95

CONTINUATION OF INVESTIGATION REPORT

CASE NUMBER	INCIDENT TYPE	PROSECUTOR'S REPORT				
G-99-	FATAL	☐ HAS BEEN SENT ☒ SUPPLEMENTARY	☐ RE-OPEN	☐ ASSIST	☒ CLOSING

4. Of further note is the fact that the deceased (　　　　) was unfamiliar with the Bridgeport area having lived in the Danbury area during his two year residency in Connecticut, and it was reported by Mrs. Flavia 　　　　 that he was constantly getting lost whenever he came into the Bridgeport area.

CONCLUSION: This Trooper's investigation concludes that the actions of Operator #1, driving the wrong way and operating under the Influence of alcohol resulted in this accident. Operator #1 is beyond enforcement.

CASE STATUS: Closed.

TFC Linda L. Johnson   10-30-99

166

TITANIUM *Woman*

DPS-633-C Rev. 7/94

STATE OF CONNECTICUT
DEPARTMENT OF PUBLIC SAFETY
DIVISION OF STATE POLICE

Case Number **G-99-**
Date **09-19-99**
Time Started **1430 Hrs.**
Time Ended **1520 Hrs.**

WITNESS STATEMENT OF **Flavia S.**

I, **Flavia S.** , date of birth

of , town /city of **Danbury, CT. 06810**

Tel.

make the following statement, without fear, threat, or promise. I have been advised that any statement(s) made herein which I do not believe to be true, and which statement is intended to mislead a public servant in the performance of his/her official function, is a crime under C.G.S section 53a-157.

On Sunday, September 19th, 1999 at approximately 06:00 AM, I received a phone call from my friend Afonso He advised me that the Danbury Police Department were at his home, 5 Cross Street in the town of Danbury. He requested for me to go over his home and speak with Danbury Police officers about our friend, Rodrigo , because he couldn't understand the officers and he didn't speak English. Upon my arrival at 5 Cross Street, I met and spoke with three Police officers. They advised me that my friend, Rodrigo had been involved in a fatal accident and that I had to go to St. Vincent Hospital in Bridgeport to identified the body.

Upon my arrival at approximately 09:00AM at St. Vincent Medical Hospital in Bridgeport with my friend, Rodson who is also a close friend of Rodrigo family. We met and spoke with a hospital staff name, Teresa. I question her about Rodrigo but she didn't have any information about the accident. She advised me to wait until someone else arrived.

Then minutes later another staff member arrived in the waiting room, escorted Robson and myself to the morgue. The person asked me several questions about our relationship with Rodrigo We advised the person that we were close friends. We then entered the morgue and saw my friend Rodrigo lying on a medical table covered with white sheets up to the neck area. I looked at his face and observed that he had sustained injuries to his facial area. I recognized a gold earring that he always wears on his left ear. We both became very upset and began to cry. We then walked out of the morgue and moments later we left the hospital, after we were able to stop crying. We then returned to our home in Danbury and notified the family back in Brasil.

No one at the hospital asked me any further questions about my friend, Rodrigo . I have known Rodrigo for approximately two (2) years since he arrived to Connecticut back in April 1997. He was living with his mother on Highland Avenue in Danbury, Connecticut. He then moved several months ago to 5 Cross Street after his mother returned to Brasil. The last time I saw Rodrigo was on Saturday, September 18th, 1999 at approximately 11:55PM or around midnight at a Miss Brasil beauty contest party on Park Avenue in Bridgeport.

By affixing my signature to this statement, I acknowledge that I have read it and/or have had it read to me and it is true to the best of my knowledge and belief.

Witness: _____ 1060   Signature _____

Witness: _____   Signature _____

Personally appeared the signer of the foregoing statement and made oath before me to the truth of the matters contained therein.

If notarized, endorse here:

Page 1 of 1 Pages.

Remerciements

Mommie-Robin Shepard

Pops-Barry Shepard

Sister Simone Shepard Turner

Sister Shandra Gregory

Nephew Jeremiah Smith ● Nephew Jahmai Gregory

Niece Tiana England ● Nephew Aaron Gregory

Auntie Burks ● Gram Shepard

Aunt Betty Pharr ● Dana Cauthen

Dominique Cauthen ● Deja Cauthen Gauthier

Deneisha Cauthen ● Father-Carlton Hanks

Uncle Mark Hanks ● Paula Hanks

Uncle Kevin Hanks ● Coretta Hanks

Aunt Elisa Brooks ● Elasia & Equan Brooks

Paternal Grandmother Zelma Hanks Wilson

Aunt Thelma ● Grandaddy Shepard

Adrian Cauthen Jr ● Beryl Kingston

Deb Bradford ● Brenda "Pete" Williams

Aunt Sandy Jackson ● Aunt Mary Shepard

Uncle Popsey Shepard ● Aunt Bonita Shepard

Aunt Carleen Shepard ● Aunt Esther Ryan

Sister Ryan ● Mika Pharr ● Godmother Benita Lee

Jim ● Val Pharr ● Duke

Robert Thompson • Cola Lawton

Kellie Milton Richardson • Dejon Dean

Kiese Milton • Shonda Roberts

Aunt Karen Chapman • Jill Day-Allegro

Sherroy Chapman • Aunt Rene Roberts

Teasha Roberts • Daivon Ballard

Lora Cauthen • Sadia Williams Douglas

Terry Shepard • Lynn Shepard • Brenda Burks

Nichelle Best • Gary Jones • Patricia Berry

Ken Berry • Linda Ryan • Ashley Ryan

Kashon Coverson • Lorrie Coverson • Marla Shepard

Aunt Sheila Miller • Jasmin Miller Luciano

Godsister Remy Miller • Minerva Thompson

Randee Thompson • Rev. Reuben Williams

Rev. Boise Kimber • Rev. Smith

Michael Jones • Tawanda Crawley Ebron

Tameeka Belcher Parks • Bud Sharpe • Aisha Sharpe

Sophia Perez • Godson Bobby Corwell

Goddaughter Phyre Corwell • Lil Popsey Shepard

Curtis Williams • Carol Shells • Addie Wardlaw

Althea Brown • Godsister Alliyah Brown

Wayne Brown • Lil Wayne Brown

Michael Amore • Jennieve Amore

Toni Payne • Rosemarie Payne • Monisa Perry

Earline Williams • Stacey"Pooh"Parker

Everett"Teddy"Thompson • Big Greg"Vader"Johnson

Aaron Washington • Chris"Pisci"Piscitelli

Denise Bentley-Drobish • Dawn Stanton-Holmes

Craig Holmes • Sheree Swann • Lorenzo Davis

David Grenade • Chief Dixon • Mr. Jim Barber

Regan Jefferson • Valencia "Vee" Edner• Jaron

Liz Xavier • Anna DePina • Lucy Sakakini

Monica Way • Lynell Camerl • Tegan DeWallace

Andi Campbell • Dian • Vicki • Junior

Deborah Caviness • Deva Caviness

Tania Davis • Piaget Davis • Barbara Curry

Theresa & Joyce • Lynn Marcella • Eric Jeffries

Sharita Madison Payton • Rita Conceico

Family Legend:

Cauthen/Ryan/Burks: *Maternal Side*

Shepard/Pharr: *(Step) Second family*

Hanks/Thompson: *Paternal Side*

TITANIUM *Woman*

Shantè T. Hanks

Shantè T. Hanks

Shantè T. Hanks

Shantè T. Hanks

Made in the USA
Middletown, DE
21 June 2021

42895080R00109